GATE
OF
HEAVEN

GATE OF HEAVEN

𝕾aint 𝕭enedict 𝕮enter

The Slaves of the Immaculate Heart of Mary

DECLARATION

In obedience to the decrees of Pope Urban VIII and other pontiffs, we declare that we submit the entire contents of this book without reserve to the judgment of the Apostolic See of the Holy roman Catholic Church.

ISBN 0-9716822-2-4

GATE OF HEAVEN is published and distributed by
The Slaves of the Immaculate Heart of Mary at Saint Benedict Center,
Post Office Box 1000, 282 Still River Road,
Still River, Massachusetts 01467,
Phone (978) 456-8296, www.saintbenedict.com

Preface

"Papal definition precludes any further interpretation of a dogma. The Church has taught from its beginning that no matter how much a doctrine may be developed or meditated upon, never, never can its meaning in any way be changed...."

The chaos, dessent and apostasy so rampant in the Church today is the direct result of the triumph of Liberalism's deceptive misrepresentation of dogmatic truth. In "Gate of Heaven," Sister Catherine Goddard Clarke reveals the deep-seated theological crisis that surfaced in the Roman Catholic Church shortly after World War II. Well-entrenched Liberalism was challenging even the sacred dogma of the Faith, "Outside the Church there is no salvation."

This power-packed book, written in 1951, is as timely and important now as it was when first published.

Editors

Contents

Chapter I

There seems to be no end to the number of reasons people can give for not facing the doctrine of the necessity of belonging to the Catholic Church for salvation.

"It is *not* the Church's doctrine," is the first difficulty.

"It is the Church's doctrine," we answer.

"None of the priests around here hold it," they make reply. "Archbishop Cushing of Boston certainly does not, nor Bishop Wright of Worcester." [1]

"That may be true," we admit, "but even so you must realize that this does not mean that No Salvation Outside the Church has ceased to be the Church's doctrine on salvation. We can give you bishops and priests over nineteen hundred years who have held this doctrine, and popes who have infallibly defined it. In fact, we can give you the whole universal Church, with all its popes and cardinals, bishops and priests."

"And whether they believe the doctrine or not, Archbishop Cushing, Bishop Wright, and the priests of the Church all over the world pronounce it every time they receive a convert into the Church, and once a week when they say their Breviary in the Sunday Office."[2]

"Is that so?" we are asked incredulously. "I find that hard

---

[1] Cushing, Richard J. (1895-1970): auxiliary bishop of Boston, 1939-44, Archbishop of Boston, 1944-70, and Cardinal from December, 1958.

Wright, John J. (1909-79): auxiliary bishop of Boston, 1947-50; first bishop of Worcester, 1950-59; bishop of Pittsburgh, 1959-69; Cardinal from 1969 and prefect of the Congregation of the Clergy, 1969-70.

[2] On August 6, 1972, the new *Liturgy of the Hours* was promulgated. The recitation of the *Athanasian Creed* is no longer part of the Office.

to believe. You may not know that parish study clubs have spent a lot of time on this question since your case came out in the newspapers. The priests lead the discussions. I don't understand why, if they say there is no salvation outside the Church on Sunday, they teach us there *is* salvation outside it on Monday."

"That is something you will have to figure out for yourself," we have ruefully to say. Every priest reads in his *Office* for Sunday the *Athanasian Creed.* Now, the Athanasian Creed begins this way:

Whosoever wishes to be saved, before all things it is necessary that he hold the Catholic Faith...Which Faith except every one do keep whole and undefiled, without doubt he shall perish eternally. Now the Catholic Faith is this...

(There follows a statement of the Creed.) The end of the Creed confirms the beginning:

This is the Catholic Faith, which except a man believe faithfully and firmly, he cannot be saved.

"What do you say to that?" we ask.

"That is pretty plain," is the answer we usually receive. "But how long has this been said in the Church?"

"From about the year 420," we reply. "Saint Athanasius himself did not write it. It was given his name because it contains the doctrines for which he suffered exile five times, and for which he was excommunicated by every Catholic Bishop in the East. For 1500 years, Catholic priests have been reciting the Creed, and have been stating at the beginning of it, and at the end of it, that there is no salvation outside the one true Church of Jesus Christ.

"And that is not all. Right in our own day, also, before a convert is received into the Catholic Church, the priest hands to him the 'Abjuration of Heresy or Profession of Faith'[3] which the convert is required to read aloud, kneeling before the priest who is to receive him. This 'Abjuration' likewise contains the doctrine of No Salvation Outside the Church. It is strong, direct and clear. This is what it says:

"I, _____ , having before me the holy Gospels, which I touch with my hand, *and knowing that no one can be saved without that faith which the Holy, Catholic, Apostolic Roman Church holds, believes, and teaches*, against which I grieve that I have greatly erred, inasmuch as I have held and believed doctrines opposed to her teaching—

"I now, with sorrow and contrition for my past errors, profess that I believe the Holy, Catholic, Apostolic Roman Church to be the only and true Church established on earth by Jesus Christ, to which I submit myself with my whole soul. I believe all the articles of Faith that she proposes to my belief, and I reject and condemn all that she rejects and condemns, and I am ready to observe all that she commands me. And I make the following profession of Faith:

(There follows the profession.)

---

[3] This is no longer part of the ritual of reception into the Church. In the new ritual, the validly baptized Christian is asked to profess the Nicene Creed, and to state: "I believe and profess all that the holy Catholic Church believes, teaches, and proclaims as revealed by God."

"And, I believe in everything else that has been defined and declared by the sacred Canons and by the General Councils, and particularly by the holy Council of Trent, and delivered, defined, and declared by the General Council of the Vatican[4], especially concerning the Primacy of the Roman Pontiff, and his infallible teaching authority.

"With a sincere heart, therefore, and with unfeigned faith, *I detest and abjure every error, heresy, and sect opposed to the said Holy, Catholic, and Apostolic Roman Church.* So help me God, and these His holy Gospels, which I touch with my hand."[5]

Our interrogator generally remains silent for a few moments after we have finished reading, and we can understand why. This is the first time he has ever heard these things. His next question, however, is revealing of the weak state of his own Faith, for, invariably, he says:

"My, that's asking a lot, isn't it? Do you mean to say people will admit all that about their former religion?"

"But it is the mere statement of the truth. Are you surprised they should speak the truth about heresy? Don't you believe heresy should be detested?"

"Yes, I suppose so; but don't you think it is rubbing it in, especially when they have been good enough to come into the Church?"

"Good enough!" we retort, "it is only right that they should accept the Truth! You are saying that they are good enough to save themselves from hell, good enough to secure themselves

---

[4] This is a reference to the First Vatican Council, 1869-70.

[5] The Priest's Ritual. Compiled by Rev. Paul Griffith, p. 47. John Murphy Company, Publishers, Baltimore, MD. 1914.

Gate of Heaven

heaven—if they live up to the Faith. Furthermore, nothing in the world could pay for the next Gift they receive, after Baptism. Have you ever been with a *real* convert when he has received his first Holy Communion?"

"No."

"We have. And if the conversion is a true one, his realization of what has happened to him is a rebuke to the apathy of lifelong Catholics. Lifelong Catholics take for granted the overwhelming Reality of Holy Communion. The convert expects enthusiasm, at least equal to his, from the older Catholic, and instead he gets wondering admiration—not that God should come to man, but that man should be good enough to come to God! This is always disillusioning and confusing to a convert, as well it might be."

"Do you supposed anyone confers a favor upon God by coming into His Church? It is the other way around."

"Yes, I suppose so."

"*Suppose* so!"

It is then we know that the Faith which is left in the American Catholic is weak, lukewarm, without fire or zest, joy or love. And then we can understand why Russia's hold is fastening every day more devilishly on Europe and the East, and threatens us. We then can understand Korea. In the ages of the Faith when, as now, the Mongol and barbarian threatened Christianity, the Catholics turned from their pleasure loving and sinful lives back to the Church. They did penance; whole nations prayed. They pilgrimaged, barefoot, to the shrines of Christendom. (They did not journey there on luxury liners.) They renewed their Faith, and made promises to God, which they kept, for the most part. And their prayers were answered. The barbarian hordes were pushed back, time and time again, just as they were about to sweep over Europe from the East, the

Southeast, and the South. They were stopped, at the gates of Vienna.[6] They were crushed, at Lepanto[7]—when we had a Saint in the Chair of Peter, Pope Pius V.

There was still enough fire in the faith of Catholics, in those days, to be rekindled. There seems to be left none at all, in our day.[8]

Our Lord told us:

Matt. 10;34: Do you think that I came to send peace upon earth: I come not to send peace, but the sword.

35: For I came to set a man at variance against his father, and the daughter against her mother, and the daughter-in-law against her mother-in-law.

36: And a man's enemies shall be they of his own household.

37: He that loveth father or mother more than me, is not worthy of me; and he that loveth son or daughter more than me, is not worthy of me.

38: And he that taketh not up his cross, and followeth me, is not worthy of me.

A modern Catholic can understand paying a price for everything but the Faith. We would have had many more supporters in our fight for the pure doctrine of Jesus Christ had not the cost been so high. One Catholic would have had to give up a job, another friends, another peace in the family, another a

---

[6] Moslem Turks assaulted Vienna, Austria, twice, the first time in 1529 and the second in 1683, when they were forced to retreat on September 12th.

[7] This was the second battle with the Moslem Turks at Lepanto. It ended in a great victory for the Catholic forces on October 7, 1571. The feast of the Most Holy Rosary was instituted to commemorate this event.

[8] It must be noted that Sister Catherine was writing ten years before the Second Vatican Council.

Gate of Heaven

political appointment, another social prestige. And being weak of faith and thoroughly self-centered themselves, Liberal Catholics find it hard to understand spiritual courage and spiritual honesty in others.

"That is not all that is required of a baptized Protestant about to enter the Church," we go on. "The instructions in *The Priest's Ritual* for a convert's reception into the Church continue:

"While the convert is still kneeling, the Priest says the *Miserere* or the *De Profundis*; after which the Priest absolves the convert from his heresy, saying: 'By the Apostolic authority, which I exercise here, I absolve *thee* from the bond of excommunication which thou hast incurred; and I restore thee to the holy Sacraments of the Church, to the communion and unity of the faithful, in the name of the Father, and of the Son, and of the Holy Ghost. Amen.' "...

I did not know for a long time—and I am sure few "cradle Catholics" are aware—that this beautiful Profession of Faith is required of non-Catholics before they are baptized conditionally. (A person is baptized unconditionally if he has never before received Baptism. Conditional Baptism is given when the convert has been baptized in some other religion, in case the first Baptism might not have been a valid one, for some reason.) All of the converts whose reception into the Church it has been our privilege to witness here at Saint Benedict Center have, by Our Lady's grace, been so conscious of the emptiness, error and confusion of the religions they were leaving that they were eager and grateful to make this

Abjuration of Heresy and Profession of Faith.

Not only do our Catholic priests recite the doctrine of No Salvation Outside the Church on the two occasions I have just given, but they read it many times in their *Office* throughout the year, in the Martyrologies. For instance, the Martyrology[9] for February 21th reads as follows:

...At Damascus[10], (in the year 743), Saint Peter Mavimeno. Some Arabs came to see him while he was ill, and to them he said, *"Whoever does not embrace the Catholic Christian religion will be damned,* as your false prophet Mohammed is"; whereupon they killed him.

The Second Nocturn in the Priest's *Office* for November 25th, relates the story of the martyrdom of Saint Catherine of Alexandria:

When she saw many diversely tormented and hauled to death by command of Maximin, because they professed the Catholic religion, she went boldly to him, and rebuking him for his savage cruelty, she affirmed with wisest reasons that *the faith of Christ is necessary for salvation.*

In the *Office* for September 27th, the feast of the Holy Martyrs, Cosmas and Damian, it is told:

---

[9] This is a reference to the Martyrology before May 9, 1969, when it was first revised since 1584 under Pope Gregory XIII. It has had a second revision since the Second Vatican Council. The newest revision was released on October 2, 2001

[10] The Moslem conquest of Syria began in the 7th Century. Unrelenting persecution and forced conversions to Islam throughout the 8th to the 14th Centuries reduced the Arab Christians from 95% to only 10% of the Syrian population. (*L'Osservatore Romano*, 9 May 2001)

...and then, for as much as they freely acknowledged themselves Catholics, and the *Catholic faith necessary for salvation,* he[11] commanded them to worship the gods, under threats of torments and a most cruel death.

These saints, no one can deny, were martyred because they held there was No Salvation Outside the Catholic Church.

The *Office* for May 4th tells the story of the Blessed Martyrs, John Cardinal Fisher, Thomas More, and their Companions, who died for the second doctrine for which Saint Benedict Center is fighting, namely, that there is no salvation without personal submission to our Holy Father, the Pope. Saint John Fisher and Saint Thomas More died, the Martyrology tells us, "strenuously fighting for the Catholic Faith and the Primacy of Peter."

While Saint Thomas More was awaiting death in the tower of London, the prosecutor for King Henry VIII came to see him. He reminded Saint Thomas More that he was being disobedient to every Catholic Bishop in England by his stubborn stand on the doctrine of the Primacy of the Pope.

"My lord," Thomas More answered him, "for one bishop of your opinion, I have a hundred saints of mine; for one parliament of yours, and God knows of what kind, I have all the General Councils of the Church for a thousand years."

It was a Pope of our day—for those who think the Church can change—who canonized Thomas More. Pope Pius XI, in 1935, canonized both Saint Thomas More and Saint John Fisher. Saint John Fisher was the Bishop who refused to follow the other Bishops of England into heresy, and who was therefore martyred, with Saint Thomas More, for the doctrine of the Primacy of the Pope and the necessity of submission to

---

[11] This was the Prefect Lysias.

him, as Christ's Vicar.

Then there is James Duckett, the heroic English bookseller, who was beatified with other English Martyrs in 1929. Blessed James Duckett was martyred on the 19th of April, 1602, in London. The Catholic book center which today, in London, bears his name, has published the story of his life and death. Of his death, the story relates:

> James Duckett showed great alacrity in his mind, and spoke boldly and cheerfully, to the astonishment of many beholders. He said of how he professed that he died a Catholic, and that so he had lived...telling the people in general that he was most willing to die for that cause, and that *it was as impossible for any to be saved outside of the Catholic Church as for any to avoid the deluge that was outside of Noah's Ark*...And so the cart was drawn from him.

We have, in the Holy Gospel according to Saint John (15;5,6) the words of Our Lord, Himself, on salvation:

> ...for without me you can do nothing. If anyone abide not in me, he shall be cast forth as a branch, and shall wither, and they shall gather him up, and cast him into the fire, and he burneth.

Saint Cyprian, the great Bishop of Carthage, who was born in the year 210 and suffered martyrdom in 258 A.D., wrote:

> The bride of Christ cannot be falsified; she is chaste and

incorrupt. She knows but one home; she with scrupulous chastity keeps inviolate her one bride chamber. She it is who preserves us for God; she finds places in the Kingdom for the children she has begotten. Whosoever separates himself from the Church is joined to an adulterer and has cut himself off from the promises made to the Church; no one who quits the Church of Christ will attain the rewards of Christ. He is a stranger, profane, an enemy. He cannot have God for his Father who has not the Church for his mother. If anyone who was outside the Ark of Noah was able to escape [and we know no one was], then whosoever is outside the Church escapes.[12]

Saint Cyprian, who was the greatest man in the Western Church from Saint Irenaeus to Saint Augustine, wrote also, in his book on the *Unity of the Church*:

If such (heretics or schismatics) should even suffer martyrdom[13] for the name of Christ, they would not expiate their crime. There can be no such thing as a martyr out of the church. Though they should be thrown into the fire, or be exposed to the fury of wild beasts, such a death will never be esteemed a crown of their faith and constancy, but rather a punishment of their perfidy. Such a man may be put to death, but cannot be crowned...If the schismatic should suffer out of the church of Christ, he will never

---

[12] *On the Unity of the Church, Treatise I:VI*

[13] The Fathers have always taught there are no martyrs outside the Church. St. Cyprian, *"De Unit.", XIV*; Saint Augustine, *Ep. 173*; Saint Eusebius, *"Hist. Eccl." V, XVI, XXI*. St Clement of Alexandria, *Strom., IV, iv*.

[14] *On the Unity of the Church, Treatise I:XIV*

thence become entitled to the recompense which none can claim who are not in it. There is but one God, one Christ, one church, one faith, and one entire body of Christian people. Whatever shall be separated from the fountain of life, can have no life remaining in it, after having lost all communication with its vital principle.[14]

Saint Jerome, the great saint and Doctor of the Church, who lived from 342 to 420, wrote to Pope Damasus:

I, following no leader save Christ, am associated in fellowship with your Blessedness, that is, with the See of Peter. On that rock I know the Church was built. Whosoever eats the Lamb outside the house is profane. If anyone shall be outside the Ark of Noah he shall perish when the flood prevails.

Saint John Chrysostom, the golden-mouthed Doctor of the Church, 347-407, speaking on the dignity of the priesthood, says:

For it is manifest folly to despise so great a ministry— without which we could obtain neither salvation nor the good things that have been promised. For as no man can enter into the kingdom of heaven, unless he be born again of water and the Holy Ghost; and except he eat the Flesh of the Lord, and drink His Blood, he shall be excluded from everlasting life; and as all these things are ministered only by the consecrated hands of priests, how could anyone without them either escape the fire of hell or obtain the crown that is prepared?

The great Bishop, Confessor and Doctor of the Church,

Saint Augustine, 354-430, who was loved and venerated in every century, said in a sermon to the people of Caesarea:

> No man can find salvation save in the Catholic Church. Outside the Catholic Church he can find everything except salvation. He can have dignities, he can have the Sacraments, can sing "Alleluia," answer "Amen," accept the Gospels, have faith in the Name of the Father, the Son and the Holy Ghost, and preach it, too, but never except in the Catholic Church can he find salvation.

Saint Augustine's writings were filled with the doctrine of No Salvation Outside the Church. He said on another occasion:

> Because we fight for the honor and unity of the Church, let us not concede to the heretics what we know to be false, but rather let us teach them by arguments that they cannot attain salvation through unity unless they come to that same unity. For the water of the Church is faithful and salutary and holy for those who use it well. *But outside of the Church no one can use it well...* Therefore we are right in censuring, anathematizing, abhorring and abominating the perversity of heart shown by heretics...

A collection of canons has come down to us from the early Church called, "Ancient Statutes of the Church." The very first of the 104 canons in this collection reads:

> He who is to be ordained bishop must first be examined whether he is prudent, teachable, of gentle manners, etc.; above all, whether he openly acknowledges the chief points of the faith, i.e. that the Father, Son, and Holy Ghost are

one God, that Christ has two natures, and yet is only one Person; whether he believes that the Old and New Testaments have only one Author and God; that the devil is not wicked by nature, but of his own free will; whether he believes in the resurrection of this flesh, and in the judgment; whether he does not disapprove marriage, or condemn second marriages, or the eating of flesh; whether he has communion with reconciled penitents, and believes that in baptism all sins, original sin as well as willful sins, are remitted, and *that extra Ecclesiam Catholicam nullus salvatur* (outside the Catholic Church no one is saved). If he passes the examination he shall be consecrated bishop, with the consent of the clergy and laity...

Saint Fulgentius, 468-533, Bishop of Ruspe, eminent among the Fathers of the Church and principal theologian of the 6th century (not counting Pope Saint Gregory the Great) writes:

Hold most firmly, and do not doubt at all, that everyone baptized outside the Catholic Church cannot be made partaker of eternal life, if before the end of this earthly life he does not return to the Catholic Church and become incorporated with it...

Hold most firmly, and do not doubt at all, that not only all the pagans, but also all the Jews, and all the heretics and schismatics who end the present life outside the Catholic Church, will go into the eternal fire, "which was prepared

---

[15] St. Fulgentius, *De Fide, ad Petrum c. 37ff., n. 78ff.* This is the quote that was used by Pope Eugenius IV in the Bull *"Cantate Domino,"* formulated at the Ecumenical Council of Florence in 1441.

for the devil and his angels." (Matt. 25;41)[15]

Pope Pelagius II, 578-590, writing to some schismatical bishops, says: "Consider therefore that whoever is not in the peace and unity of the Church cannot have God."

Pope Innocent III, in 1208, in a "Profession of Faith" prescribed to the Waldensians says:

> With our hearts we believe and with our lips we confess but one Church, not that of the heretics, but the Holy Roman Catholic and Apostolic Church, outside which we believe that no one is saved.

Saint Thomas Aquinas (1225-1274) teaches throughout his writings that it is necessary to belong to the one true Church of Jesus Christ in order to be saved. In his treatise *Against the Errors of the Greeks*, Saint Thomas wrote:

> To be subject to the Roman Pontiff is necessary for salvation.

Saint Bonaventure, a Doctor of the Church who lived in the same century with Saint Thomas Aquinas, and who died in the same year (1274), says in his *Breviloquium*:

> Because outside of the unity of faith and love which makes us sons and members of the Church, no one can be saved, hence if the Sacraments are received outside the Church, they are not effective for salvation, although they are true Sacraments. However, they can become useful if one returns to Holy Mother the Church, the only Spouse of Christ, whose sons alone Christ the Spouse deems worthy

of eternal inheritance.

Pope Clement VI, in the fourteenth century, writing to the Armenian Patriarch, says:

We ask if you believe, and the Armenians obedient to you, that no man of those travelling outside the faith of the same Church and the obedience to the Pontiff of the Romans can finally be saved;...if you have believed and believe that all those who set themselves up against the faith of the Roman Church and died in final impenitence will be damned and descend to the perpetual torments of hell.

Pope Pius IV, in the sixteenth century, speaks of "this true Catholic faith, outside of which no one can be saved."

Two of the three sixteenth century saints who were made Doctors of the Church were Jesuits. They were Saint Peter Canisius (1521-1597), and Saint Robert Bellarmine (1542-1621). Both these Doctors professed again and again the doctrine of no salvation outside the one true Church, nor without personal submission to Christ's Vicar, the Roman Pontiff. And, like every saint, both were devoted children of Christ's Mother. Saint Peter Canisius wrote a *Catechism* of Catholic doctrine. In his Catechism, he says:

Outside of this communion (as outside of the Ark of Noah) there is absolutely no salvation for mortals: not to Jews or Pagans, who never received the faith of the Church; not to heretics who, having received it, forsook or corrupted it; not to schismatics who left the peace and unity of the Church; finally neither to excommunicates who for any other serious cause deserved to be put away and separated from the body of the Church, like pernicious members...For the rule of Cyprian and Augustine is certain: he will not have God for his Father who would not have the Church for his Mother.

Saint Peter Canisius in his *Catechism* asks: "Who is to be called a Christian?" And he answers:

He who confesses the salutary doctrine of Jesus Christ, true God and true Man, in His Church. Hence, he who is truly a Christian condemns and detests thoroughly all cults and sects which are found outside the doctrine the Church of Christ, everywhere, and among all peoples, as for example, the Jewish, the Mohammedan, and the heretical cults and sects; and he firmly assents to the same doctrine of Christ.

How far away from their two Doctors the Society of Jesus has gone in our day is seen in the dismissal of Father Leonard Feeney by the Jesuits[16], for holding in exactly the way Saint Peter Canisius held it, the Church's doctrine on salvation. Father Feeney has never ceased to be devoted to these two Jesuit Doctors of the Church and to the Jesuit Saints, most especially Saint Ignatius, Saint Aloysius, and Saint Francis Xavier. It was the Society of Jesus as these men founded and lived it that Father thought he had joined, at seventeen years of age. When he found the modern Jesuits preaching a doctrine on salvation which was the opposite of the one preached by Saint Peter Canisius and Saint Robert Bellarmine, he sadly allowed himself to be dismissed. He knew in his heart that he was being

---

[16] The dismissal date was October 10, 1949.

loyal to Saint Ignatius and the early saints of his Order by doing so.

Two of the most beautiful pictures which hang on the walls of Saint Benedict Center, are of Saint Ignatius Loyola and Saint Aloysius Gonzaga. They were painted especially for Father Feeney by two members of the Center. One of the Center houses is named Saint Francis Xavier, the great Jesuit apostle to the Indies.

The Jesuit saint, Robert Bellarmine, who strongly defends the doctrine that Outside the Catholic Church No One can be Saved, defines the Catholic Church as:

> The congregation of men bound together by the profession of the same Christian Faith, and by the communion of the same Sacraments, under the rule of the legitimate pastors, and especially of the one Vicar of Christ on earth, the Roman Pontiff.

In the eighteenth century, Pope Benedict XIV, in a profession of faith prescribed to the Orientals, writes of:

> ...this faith of the Catholic Church, outside of which no one can be saved.

In the nineteenth century, Pope Gregory XVI, in his famous encyclical against Felicite de Lamennais, writes:

> Now we set forth another most fruitful cause of evils, by which we bewail that the Church is at present afflicted, namely, Indifferentism, or that perverse opinion, which has become prevalent by the deceit of the wicked, from all sides: that, by whatever profession of faith, the eternal

salvation of the soul can be attained, if one's morals conform to the norm of a right and honest life...

In the nineteenth century, also, Pope Pius IX published his *Syllabus of Modern Errors*. Pope Pius IX was writing against the Indifferentists. The Indifferentists of the nineteenth century have become the Liberals of the twentieth century, and their doctrines are the false teachings which Saint Benedict Center is fighting today. Pope Pius IX declared—in the Syllabus of Modern Errors:

> *It is error to believe that*: 16. "Men can, in the cult of any religion, find the way of eternal salvation and attain eternal salvation."
> *It is error to believe that*: 17. "One ought at least to have good hope for the eternal salvation of all those who in no way dwell in the true Church of Christ."
> *It is error to believe that*: 18. "Protestantism is nothing else than a different form of the same Christian religion, in which, equally as in the Catholic Church, it is given to please God."

A year before the turn of the twentieth century (on January 22, 1899), Pope Leo XIII published an encyclical letter, "Testem Benevolentiae," addressed to His Eminence, Cardinal Gibbons, Archbishop of Baltimore. The entire stand of Saint Benedict Center, in the Boston Heresy Controversy, is stated here in this encyclical of Pope Leo XIII. Here, it may be said, is our grievance and our plea, all in one.

Pope Leo XIII writes that some Catholics in America teach that:

> ...in order the more easily to bring over to Catholic doctrine those who dissent from it, the Church ought to

adapt herself somewhat to our advanced civilization, and, relaxing her ancient rigor, show some indulgence to modern popular theories and methods. Many think that this is to be understood not only with regard to the rule of life, but also to the doctrines in which the Deposit of Faith is contained. For they contend that it is opportune, in order to work in a more attractive way upon the wills of those who are not in accord with us, to pass over certain heads of doctrines, as if of lesser moment, or to so soften them that they may not have the same meaning which the Church has invariably held. Now, Beloved Son, few words are needed to show how reprehensible is the plan that is thus conceived, if we but consider the character and origin of the doctrine which the Church hands down to us. On that point the Vatican Council[17] says: "The doctrine of faith which God has revealed is not proposed like a theory of philosophy which is to be elaborated by the human understanding, but as a divine deposit delivered to the Spouse of Christ to be faithfully guarded and infallibly declared....That sense of the sacred dogmas is to be faithfully kept which Holy Mother Church has once declared, and is not to be departed from under the specious pretext of a more profound understanding."[18] Far be it, then, for any one to diminish or for any reason whatever to pass over anything of this divinely delivered doctrine; whosoever would do so, would rather wish to alienate Catholics from the Church than to bring over to the Church those who dissent from it. Let them return; indeed, nothing is nearer to Our heart; let all those who are wandering far

---

[17] This refers to the First Vatican Council 1869-70.

[18] Vatican I (Const. de Fid. cath. c. iv.)

from the sheepfold of Christ return; but let it not be by any other road than that which Christ has pointed out.

The Sacred Congregation of the Propagation of the Faith, under Blessed Pius X[19], in 1907, in answer to a question as to whether Confucius could have been saved, wrote:

It is not allowed to affirm that Confucius was saved. Christians, when interrogated, must answer that those who die as infidels are damned.

•   •   •   •   •   •   •   •

The above are *statements* of the doctrines of No Salvation Outside the Church, nor without personal submission to the Pope. There follow the *infallible definitions* of the Popes on the Church's doctrine on salvation. These definitions must be believed under pain of excommunication. I have taken them directly from the *Enchiridion Symbolorum*. The *Enchiridion Symbolorum*, or *The Handbook of the Creed*, contains all the major pronouncements of the Popes—either defining alone or at the head of their bishops in Council—and all the *ex cathedra* definitions. The theologians refer to the *Enchiridion* usually as "Denzinger." It was compiled by Henricus Denzinger.[20]

The following, then, are the *ex cathedra* definitions of the Popes on No Salvation Outside the Catholic Church, nor without submission to the Holy Roman Pontiff:

---

[19] Beatified in 1951 and canonized May 29,1954.

[20] In the years following the writing of this book, *Denzinger* was edited by a Fr. Karl Rahner, S.J., a "Universalist" (one who believes that all will go to Heaven). Fr. Rahner inserted certain non-authoritative statements which would further the propagation of this heretical belief.

The Fourth Lateran Council, in 1215, under Pope Innocent III, defining against the Albigenses and other heretics, declared:

There is but one universal Church of the faithful, outside of which no one at all can be saved. (Denz. No. 430)

Pope Bonifice VIII, 1294-1303, in his bull, *Unam Sanctam*, Nov. 18, 1302, expounds the doctrine of the Church and ends with an infallible definition:

Urged by faith, We are obliged to believe and to hold that the Church is one, holy, catholic, and also apostolic. We firmly believe in her, and We confess absolutely that outside of her there is neither salvation nor the remission of sins, as the Spouse in the Canticles (VI, 8) proclaims: "One is my dove, my perfect one. She is the only one of her mother, the chosen of her that bore her," who represents one mystical body, whose head is Christ, and the head of Christ is God. In her there is one Lord, one faith, one baptism. There was indeed at the time of the deluge only one Ark of Noah, prefiguring the One Church, which Ark, having been finished to a single cubit, had only one pilot and guide, i.e. Noah, outside of which, as we read, all that subsisted on earth was destroyed....

Furthermore, *We declare, say define and pronounce, that it is wholly necessary for the salvation of every human creature to be subject to the Roman Pontiff.* (Denz. Nos. 468, 469)

Pope Eugene IV, in the Council of Florence, decreed in the Bull Cantate Domino, February 4, 1441:

The most Holy Roman Church firmly believes, professes

and preaches, that *none of those existing outside the Catholic Church, not only pagans, but also Jews and heretics and schismatics, can have a share in life eternal*; but that they will go into the eternal fire, "which was prepared for the devil and his angels," unless before death they are joined with Her; and that so important is the unity of this ecclesiastical body that only those remaining within this unity can profit by the sacraments of the Church unto salvation, and they alone can receive an eternal recompense for their fasts, their almsgiving, their other works of Christian piety, and the duties of a Christian soldier. No one, let his almsgiving be as great as it may, *no one, even if he pour out his blood for the name of Christ, can be saved, unless he remain within the bosom and the unity of the Catholic Church.*

Surely, if language is to mean anything at all, and if we are to retain even the most basic kind of sanity—the sanity which preserves for us the fact that two and two are four, black is black, and white is white, and that a thing cannot be both true and false at the same time—we will know that this infallible definition of Pope Eugene can have but one meaning—that which it so clearly states. To repeat:

None of those existing outside the Catholic Church, not only pagans, but also Jews and heretics and schismatics, can have a share in eternal life....No one, even if he pour out his blood for the name of Christ, can be saved unless he remain within the bosom and the unity of the Catholic Church.

Any one of the hundreds of thousands of Catholics who have gone, like faithful children, to their priests, after the Boston Heresy Case brought the question of salvation into the headlines of newspapers all over the world, will remember that instead of the strong, unmistakable teaching of the Church, speaking through Pope Eugene IV, their priests taught them some one of the following astounding *errors* and *distortions*:

(1) Any pagan, Jew, heretic or schismatic *can* be saved, while remaining outside the Catholic Church, by reasons of his own sincerity and his own virtues.

Comment: No comment.

(2) There is a substitute for the reception of the Body, Blood, Soul and Divinity of our Lord and Saviour, Jesus Christ, in Holy Communion! This substitute is the living of a naturally moral life—without the Sacraments—along with a desire to do God's will and go to heaven.

Comment: This "desire to do God's will" is a vague thing, an orthodox inquirer will discover, and it violently rejects Christ's will that all men should come to a knowledge of the Church—in His Church.

(3) A man, even though he himself angrily resents and denies he is, or ever would *become*, a Catholic, can be saved because he "implicitly" belongs to the Church.

Comment: No one as yet as been able to explain quite what this means, or how it is brought about. We believe the concept blasphemous and silly.

(4) Many people who are totally ignorant of Christ and His Church can be saved because their ignorance excuses them and confers on them baptism of desire.

Comment: They are ignorant of the Church, we inquire, and yet they desire it? They are ignorant of Baptism and Holy

Eucharist, and yet they desire these life-giving Sacraments? As I will bring out in another chapter, this type of reasoning on the part of Catholics is a denial of the Goodness and the Power of God (a) to provide no means, or (b) to be unable to find means, of getting the Gospel to men of such good will—in this day of airplane and radio, when even business men, like Coca Cola manufacturers, manage to advertise their products everywhere in the world, and the American motion pictures have invaded the jungles.

(5) Many intelligent Americans in our day can be saved while refusing the Catholic Church because (a) they are invincibly ignorant, or (b) they have not the gift of Faith.

Comment: (a) "Invincible ignorance" in this case seems to have come to mean: *hopelessly incapable of understanding.* Since even little children can grasp the Faith, invincible ignorance must be a most dense form of stupidity. Saint Benedict Center is situated across the street from Harvard University. Liberal Catholics, at haste to protect the majority of Harvard faculty members and students from our denunciation of them as atheistic, agnostic, and heretical, have declared them to be, rather, simply "invincibly ignorant." We do not think Harvard would be happy about this distinction, but might, on the other hand, prefer our appraisal of them as being "invincibly proud."

(b) The awarding of heaven to those who remain outside the Church because "they have not the gift of Faith," is made in spite of the fact that the gift of Faith *has* been bestowed, once and for all, and is waiting to be accepted—in any Catholic Church or rectory. Non-Catholics simply refuse to accept it. And yet modern theologians teach that, nevertheless, these non-Catholics can be saved. For this false teaching, we hold that the theologians themselves will not be saved.

(6) There are many ways of getting to heaven. The Catholic Church is merely the *surest* way. The Catholic Church may, in fact, be likened to an ocean liner; the other churches to rowboats, or sailboats, or even motorboats. These latter will get there, but they are not as safe conveyances as the ocean liner.

Comment: If that is the case, no church is entirely sure of getting us there. I have known ocean liners that have gone beautifully to the bottom of the sea. The Catholic Church cannot be said, in any sense, to be the "surest way." It must be said to be *the only way*. For that is the stark truth.

If the above simile could hold up at all (which it cannot), imagine wanting to send anyone you love across the ocean in a rowboat; or even in a motorboat (with no gas stations on the way!) And imagine this being God's plan for ocean crossing, from the shores of time to the shores of eternity!

Papal definition precludes any further interpretation of a dogma. The Church has taught from its beginning that no matter how much a doctrine may be developed or meditated upon, never, never can its meaning in any way be changed. Despite all this, bishops, priests, theologians, and canon lawyers in our day have insisted that distinctions be made with regard to the solemn doctrine "Outside the Church there is no Salvation." These distinctions are so involved, confused, fantastic and dishonest that the dogma finally has emerged—in the minds of the Faithful—as completely changed. To the straightforward question: Is there or is there not salvation outside the Catholic Church? the answer, after this manipulation of doctrine, would have to be: *Yes*; there *is* salvation outside the Catholic Church. We have arrived now at the exact opposite of the *ex cathedra* pronouncements of the Popes.

Perhaps the following account will best illustrate to what crazy lengths this sinful tampering with doctrine has gone in our day.

In one of Saint Benedict Center's houses, the telephone rang, on an evening in late August, 1950. The members of Saint Benedict Center were at dinner. The telephone call was from the United Press, in Boston.

"May we speak with Father Feeney, please?" someone at the other end of the line asked. "Pope Pius XII has just come out with an encyclical in which he states the doctrine you have been fighting for. We would like to get a statement from Father Feeney."

"Yes, I will give you a statement if I think one is called for," Father answered, "Can you send someone around to the Center in an hour with the text of the Holy Father's message?"

"I will get you a text, Father," the United Press man said, "but I can read to you now exactly what the Pope said about 'your' doctrine."

"Yes, read it," Father asked.

"The Pope says: 'Some reduce to a meaningless formula the necessity of belonging to the True Church in order to gain salvation.'"

"Thank you," Father said, "I will see you at the Center."

Later on, the *New York Times* telephoned, and asked for Father Feeney.

"We have the translation of the Pope's encyclical, *Humani Generis*," the *Times* man said, "and we have checked his pronouncement on no salvation outside the Church with the release you gave us when you were silenced. In that release you said theologians today are making the doctrines of the Church absolutely meaningless. Did you know the Pope says the same thing in this new encyclical? He says, 'Some reduce to a meaningless formula the necessity of belonging to the True Church in order to gain salvation.' Will you give us a statement?"

The editions of the *New York Times* for the next day carried Father Feeney's statement, and newspapers all over the United States printed the United Press release of Father's story of his joy and relief—for the salvation of souls—at the Holy Father's confirmation of the Church's solemn doctrine.

The Protestant world had no doubt as to the meaning of the Pope's warning. But the Catholic world did—thanks to the theologians appointed to interpret for Catholics the hidden meaning of the Holy Father's seemingly obvious message. Catholic comment, when finally it broke forth, lacked the direct and frank simplicity of the secular writing. The Catholic analysis was full of the same weird complexity, confused and twisted evasion that marked the articles written before the Pope's encyclical, and after the Boston Heresy Case.

The *Denver Register*, a Catholic newspaper; *The Sign*, a Catholic magazine; and all the Paulists' publications were guilty of this same treatment of sacred dogma. It remained, however, for the *American Ecclesiastical Review*, the most eminent of them all, to turn things so entirely topsy-turvy, to make such a complete departure from sanity and common sense that for an hour after we first read their article our heads reeled. We became very angry, to think that churchmen could dare think, much less print, such blasphemy against Revealed Truth.

What happened was this: A friend brought us two copies of the February and March (1951) issues of the *American Ecclesiastical Review*, containing a long article on the doctrine of No Salvation Outside the Church by the Rev. Joseph Clifford Fenton, D.D., of Catholic University, editor of the magazine. In the continued article, Father Fenton attacked Father Feeney, Raymond Karam, and Saint Benedict Center, on their stand on the doctrinal controversy in which they are engaged. He spoke of the Holy Father's censure, in the encyclical *Humani Generis*, of those who reduce the dogma "Outside the Church there is No Salvation" to a meaningless formula. And now comes the shock: According to Father Fenton, the people who reduce the doctrine to a meaningless formula—are Father Feeney and Saint Benedict Center!

And what is it Father Feeney and Saint Benedict Center are saying about the doctrine which makes it meaningless? They are saying it means *exactly what it says*.

At this point, dear reader, before our heads spin again, perhaps we had better leave the subject, and go on with something else.

Afterthought before departure: If, when the Holy Father makes a pronouncement, we cannot be sure what he means, but must wait until his words are explained to us by such teachers as Father Fenton and Father Connell, of Catholic University— when Father Fenton and Father Connell have spoken, how can we be sure what *they* mean? If the Holy Father's utterances are not clear, what title have these un-infallible teachers to be the safeguards of clarity? As an old Indian proverb used to say, "Ali Baba will go bail for Abou Rah, but who will go bail for Ali Baba?"

Chapter II

One of the purposes of this book is to make a filial and loving appeal to the American Catholic Bishops. It is to entreat them to go back to teaching us once more the dogmas of our Holy Faith as they were given to the Church by Our Lord, Jesus Christ, through His Apostles, and as they have been taught throughout the ages.

The story of Saint Benedict Center and its fight for doctrine is told in *The Loyolas and The Cabots*, the account of the Boston Heresy Case. Many who have read this book have written or telephoned the Center to ask what has happened to us since the day in 1949 when our story ended in *The Loyolas and The Cabots*. Many have said, too, that they wish I had written at more length on the doctrines which are the basis for the controversy in the so-called Boston Heresy Case.

And so, as well as being an appeal to the Catholic Bishops of America, this book is a statement of our doctrinal position, put in the simple form a layman is bound to write in, with, perhaps, the added advantage of a year more of study. We have had a good deal of time in which to study, during the two years we have been cut off from the world. We live, it might almost be said, in a little Catholic ghetto.

These past two years have been ones not only of study, but of persecution—unbelievable persecution. However, persecution has never been known to hurt the Faith. It has hurt us, it is true, but this has been pain which has purged our souls, as it healed them.

We have had rich blessings from the Blessed Mother of God. She has given us a deeper knowledge of her Son and His Church. We have been able to defend her against her enemies,

Gate of Heaven

on Boston Common. When Archbishop Cushing interdicted[21] us—which by the way is a different penalty from excommunication, though no Boston Catholic knew, or was told how to distinguish this—the crowds which used to flock to Saint Benedict Center began to diminish. We realized then that it was time for us to go out into the highways and the byways, and we selected as our highway the central mall on Boston Common. Every Sunday afternoon, rain or shine, Father Leonard Feeney and the boys of Saint Benedict Center are to be found professing their Catholic Faith from this spot on the Common.[22]

We have had an inestimable blessing, during these past two years, in the company and inspiration of a brave and devoted priest—in a battle against odds so overwhelming that were we to stop to count them we would be overcome with fear for him. We never had fear, thanks be to God, either for Father Feeney or for ourselves. Somehow, Our Lady has always sustained us. We even seem to borrow from her at times, for weak and poor and harassed and little as we are, every now and then, like our Queen, we actually feel "terrible as an army set in array." We seem to sense her anger at the murderous things being done to her Son in the world. Her vast sadness fills our souls, and it is in those moments that we think our voice could reach to the ends of the earth. We know from what her anguish stems.

And so we have had no personal fear through all the things that have happened to us as a result of our teaching that it is a defined doctrine of the Catholic Church that there is no

---

[21] Interdict: The deprivation of the Sacraments and liturgical activities.

[22] They did this from July 23, 1950 (Feast of Saint Apollinaris of Ravenna) to January 30, 1958 (Feast of Saint Martina), when the community moved to Still River, Massachusetts.

salvation outside it, nor without personal submission to our Holy Father, the Pope. We have taught that this dogma, like all defined dogmas, must be taken to mean literally just what it says, and that it cannot be interpreted in such a way as to change its meaning. Such a change would constitute heresy.

At the end of this book, for those who have inquired and those who are interested, I will give, in as much detail as I am able, the story of what we are doing at present.

Each of us has had, along with the sufferings which befell us as a group, some personal renunciation to make in the way of family and old friends. These renunciations have, in almost every case, been heartbreaking and hard. One of our members, a gentle and sensitive girl, had to face the knowledge, as she sat with us in the Cambridge Criminal Court, that we were there: the first time because of the trumped-up malice of her father; and the second time because of the equally trumped-up malice of her mother.

One of the miscreants we discovered sitting in the courtroom with us, but inside the enclosure provided for those whose nocturnal adventures are, for the most part, alcoholically inspired, was Jeff, a harmless and lovable old character who lives in our neighborhood. It is impossible not to like old Jeff, in spite of his shortcomings. He has an ageless, shaggy look, and whenever he sees Father Feeney coming, he whips off his hat, snaps himself into what would pass, with him, for attention, and begins to recite—the Hail Mary.

This morning of which I speak, Jeff spotted Father, sitting amongst us in the courtroom. His eyes became sheepish, and his face flushed. He sat up, very straight. And there, on the lapel of his coat, the same as on ours, was the medal of Our Lady of the Bowed Head which Father Feeney had pinned there one morning when Jeff had come to tell him his troubles.

We all saw it at once. Father Feeney's face lit up. There came into his eyes love for his elderly child across the room in the enclosure. Jeff felt it, and when finally he pigeon-toed out, as is his way, he chose the exit close to where Father was sitting. He did not look up as he passed, nor did he speak, but he eloquently rubbed, with the end of his shabby sleeve, the little medal on his coat lapel. The tragedy of our being there went out of our hearts. We were light-hearted and joyous again. We had no reputation to lose. That had been lost long ago, for Our Lady. And we knew, no matter how futile it proved for us to try to tell our story in a court or before a board, Our Lady would this time, as always, protect us.

The matter which brought us on this particular morning to the Cambridge Criminal Court was more serious even than our case before the Supreme Court of Massachusetts. We had pleaded before the Supreme Court that our G.I. Bill be not taken away from the veterans attending our school. Saint Benedict Center School had had without question the approval of the State Board of Collegiate Authority for nine terms. When we publicly defended a defined doctrine of the Catholic Church that there is no salvation outside it, and we were, as a result of this defense, placed under religious interdict, our G.I. Bill was first threatened, and then finally taken away from us.

We were in the Cambridge Criminal Court because our enemies had found a way at last to violate the privacy of Father Feeney's home, through the city officials of Cambridge. The pretext was a letter (our lawyer called it a "poison pen letter") which was written by a woman whose husband had tried to use the city offices against us a year before. She complained that Father's house is old (it *is* on the edge of the slums, but the Center boys, by their own labor, have reinforced it.) She listed the door which opened in, instead of out (she was worried about fire, so she said). She recounted the bathing facilities (she did not know there were none when Fakhri and Mary Maluf first found the house, three years before, during Cambridge's housing shortage, and that most of Father's neighbors have no bathrooms or hot water).

She built up her story, against a harassed, persecuted Catholic priest, silenced and smeared in the newspapers of the world for Catholic doctrine, without a fair hearing or a real chance to defend himself. She built up her evidence, purported to have been obtained from a man Father Feeney had shortly before befriended. And finally she stated that, way in the recesses of the old house, so she was told, Father Feeney was privately—saying his daily Mass.

That is why we sat that morning in the Cambridge Criminal Court. We had refused, from such malevolent testimony, to allow an inspector to enter Father Feeney's home.

It is true that ten years ago, at Saint Benedict Center, we were not talking as strongly upon doctrine as we are now. We were, at that time, as a matter of fact, unaware of many things which we are painfully aware of now. Father Leonard Feeney then was the well-known and greatly loved Jesuit poet, essayist, lecturer and teacher. Every priest and nun in this country and in England knew and admired his writings. The nuns used them in the schools. His earlier poems the children were taught to memorize. His essays, stories, and later poems were studied by students in secondary schools and Catholic colleges.

Father Feeney's mother and father have told me that no matter where they were traveling, in the United States or in Europe, in the course of the journey some person they met was sure to ask: "Are you Father Leonard Feeney's parents? Your son's books have given me many pleasant hours." Or, "Will

Gate of Heaven

you tell Father Leonard that I met a fellow on a train once who was a double for his Charlie Maloney, in *Fish on Friday?*" Or, "Say, Mr. Feeney, the school master in my home was the image of the old master your son tells about in Skheenarinka!"

Once, in California, a young priest came to Father Feeney's room and asked him if he would come over to the sick-bed of his mother. She was dying, the young priest said, and all her life she had prayed that when she was dying Father Feeney would be with her, to say for her her favorite poem.

Father actually stood at the bedside of his unknown friend, and in the presence of her priest son and her nurse, he recited, to the very end, the poem of his which she loved so much. It was:

Angela died to-day and went to Heaven;
  We counted her summers up and they were seven.
But why does that trouble you, unloosened shutter,
  That flap at my window in the wind's wild flutter!

Angela's eyes to-night are cold and dim,
  Off in the land of song and Seraphim.
But what does that mean to you, O creaking stair,
  And mice in the wall that gnaw the plaster there!

Angela's little hands are folded white,
  Deep in the meadow, under the starry night.
But why should an ugly gnat keep finely whining
  Around the candle-flame beside me shining!

And never again—and never again will she
  Come running across the field to welcome me.
But, little sheep-bells, out on the distant hill,

Why, at this hour, do you wake and tinkle still!

And not any more—alas!—and not any more,
 Will she climb the stairs and knock at my lonely door.
But, moaning owl in the hayloft overhead,
 How did you come to know that she was dead![23]

This took place in Los Angeles, California, in the Hospital of the Holy Angels.

Father Feeney entered the Jesuit Order when he was seventeen years old, from his home in Lynn, Massachusetts. He had two younger brothers and a sister. His two younger brothers became priests, also, one a Jesuit and the other a secular priest. Father's mother and father are still living, thank God. They have both been a source of strength and joy to us during what would have been, for most parents, a time of humiliation. They have suffered with us, but always gallantly and nobly. They were taught "our" doctrine as children, and they never doubted our cause was any other than that of the Blessed Mother of God, for the protection of the Church of her Divine Son.

After he had made his Jesuit studies in America, Father Feeney was sent to England and France for further study. When he returned to the United States, he taught in the Graduate School at Boston College, and from there he was sent to New York, to be Literary Editor of *America*[24], the national Jesuit weekly. Father spent four years in New York, writing, editing,

---

[23] Night Noises, from *In Towns and Little Towns*, America Press, 1927

[24] Fr.Feeney served in that position from June 6, 1936 to October 5, 1940.

Gate of Heaven

lecturing—part of the intellectual life of a great city.

Cardinal Hayes[25], of New York, was his friend, and so was Monsignor Lavelle, the Vicar General of the Archdiocese. Father gave the course of sermons for Advent, in Saint Patrick's Cathedral. He lectured to Catholic audiences in New York, and from there went off for lectures all over the country.

He confessed, however, to being lonely for parish work, such as he had done in Manchester, England, while he was studying there. And so he found a small apostolate for himself among the taxicab drivers, in New York City. These friends have never left him. They have remained faithful to this day.

Father found work to do also among college students. His message to both groups was exactly the same. It is Father Feeney's message to everybody: the Holy Catholic Church for salvation; the Son of God in the Holy Eucharist for adoration; and Mary, God's Mother, for our Mother.

This is Father's message today, at Saint Benedict Center. (Father Feeney came to Weston College from New York, and to Saint Benedict Center from Weston College.) His message has never changed. He gave it in New York, made notable conversions by it, and was praised and admired. He gives it in Boston—very much stronger, I grant, for the times have grown more evil, but the same message nevertheless—and now he is punished for it. He is silenced, and Saint Benedict Center is put under interdict. But it is the same message.

There is one difference, it is true; a very significant one. Father Feeney preached the same message, and we all preach it, at Saint Benedict Center, in challenge to the godless teaching of Harvard University. Father Feeney made many conversions at Harvard College, and a number of students resigned from

---

[25] Cardinal Hayes, of New York – Hayes, Patrick J. (1867-1938): auxiliary bishop of New York, 1914-19; Archbishop of New York, 1919-38, and Cardinal from 1924.

Harvard as a result of these conversions. Now this is a serious thing to bring about, in the most powerful university in America, even though a Catholic priest is ordained for just such a purpose. A Catholic priest is ordained to save men from the occasions of sin, and from all that threatens their eternal salvation.

Archbishop Cushing and Bishop Wright, finally, were invited, on separate evenings, to Harvard, for dinner. Influential Harvard Catholics, anxious to preserve social prestige for the Church, exerted pressure in the right places. And so Father Feeney, when Archbishop Cushing and Bishop Wright were out at sea on a pilgrimage (both had promised us a hearing should anything threaten us), was transferred out of the diocese[26], to Holy Cross College in Worcester, to teach English.

Another Jesuit, despite our protest, was assigned to Saint Benedict Center. He was to get out of our heads what Father Feeney had put into them. He was to preach, by manner and by doctrine, a message less embarrassing to Harvard College and to social Liberal Catholics than the blunt, honest, unequivocal doctrine of Jesus Christ, for which the martyrs had died and the saints suffered.

We prevailed upon Father to give us his protection by remaining with us, at least until we were given the hearing which Archbishop Cushing and Bishop Wright had promised us. We convinced him that he was in conscience bound to remain with his children in a doctrinal crisis of such serious nature.

Father remained with us, knowing full well that it might mean the sacrifice of everything in his life that he held dear: his reputation as a completely devoted and zealous priest; the love

---

[26] August 25,1948

of little children who knew him through his poetry; the apostolate of his writing; the comfort, in their last years, of his parents; and service in that Society which he had entered thirty-four years before. He offered it all to the Mother of God, and she accepted it. Father remained with us, and in Holy Week of the same year[27], the whole thing came to a head. Four courageous and strong Catholic teachers, Fakhri Maluf, James Walsh, Charles Ewaskio, and David Supple, were dismissed from their positions at Boston College and Boston College High School for teaching the defined doctrines of the Church that there is no salvation outside it, nor without personal submission to our Holy Father, the Pope. The Boston Heresy Case, so-called, went out all over the world.

And so we come back to where we started. This book is written to make a filial and loving appeal to the American Catholic Bishops. It is to tell them that we are worried because they seem to be so busy establishing their reputations as good Americans that they do not have time to maintain the dogmas that preserve our Holy Faith. We have even come to wonder if they know the doctrines. It appears that the Holy Father may be wondering about this, too. He as much as said so, in his encyclical, *Humani Generis*, released on August 21, 1950, when he declared concerning his sons, the Bishops:

43: Some reduce to a meaningless formula the necessity of belonging to the True Church in order to gain salvation....

44: These and like errors, it is clear, have crept in among certain of our sons who are deceived by imprudent zeal for souls or by false science. To them We are compelled with grief to repeat once again truths already well known and to point out

---

[27] April, 1949

with solicitude clear errors and dangers of error.

It is no particular virtue on the part of Cardinal Spellman of New York[28], Archbishop Cushing of Boston, or any of our Bishops, that they are good Americans. That is to be expected of them. We would, however, say that we have no need of their leadership in politics. Men have been duly elected, from President Truman down to the least office holder, to take care of that function for us.

We do have need of the guardianship of our Faith by our Bishops. We have need of their preservation of the Faith for us, exactly as it came from Jesus Christ through His Apostles, with no innovations. That is, with no new additions or interpretations made at the expense of doctrine, in order to appease Protestants and Jews.

Let us take up, first, the question which our American Bishops seem anxious to avoid answering. That question is this: Are those that are saved many, or are they few?

In view of the fact that Catholics are in a minority in America—they are only about one-sixth of the population[29]— for diplomatic or political reasons, our Bishops do not want either to answer or to force this question. But it is one which must be answered if the Gospel is to be preached, and souls are to be saved.

---

[28] Cardinal Spellman of New York – Spellman, Francis J. (1889-1967): auxiliary bishop of Boston, 1932-39; Archbishop of New York, 1939-67 and Cardinal from 1946.

[29] As of July 1, 2001, the population of the United States was 284,796,887 (U.S. Census Bureau). As of 2001 the Catholic population living in the United States was 63,683,030 (2002 Catholic Almanac). This would put the Catholic populous at almost 4.5 percent of the total population.

"Are there few that are saved, Lord?" asked a certain man of Jesus.

And Jesus answered—that few are saved.

"Strive to enter by the narrow gate," He said, "for many, I say to you, shall seek to enter, and shall not be able....

"You shall begin to stand without, and knock at the door, saying: Lord, open to us. And he answering, shall say to you: I know you not, whence you are.

"Then you shall begin to say: We have eaten and drunk in thy presence...And he shall say to you: I know you not, whence you are: depart from me, all ye workers of iniquity.

"There shall be weeping and gnashing of teeth, when you shall see Abraham and Isaac and Jacob, and all the prophets, in the kingdom of God, and you yourselves thrust out." (Luke 13; 23-28)

Now this is the "gentle Jesus" speaking. Father Feeney, in imitation of Jesus, speaks like this every Sunday on Boston Common. The Liberal Catholics, Protestants, and Jews, listening to him, almost with one voice cry: "Preach *love*, brother! Jesus preached *love*! You are preaching *hate*!"

Father Feeney's answer is: "Jesus preached love—of His Eternal Father. He did not preach love for those who deny His Word. For these He preached eternal damnation."

Mary, God's Mother, whose picture is on the stand behind Father Feeney as he talks, herself admonished the three Fatima children to pray unceasingly, because vast thousands of souls were being lost. She permitted the children a glimpse of hell, in an apparition, and little Jacinta could talk of nothing else, for the short while she lived.

"Oh, if I could only show them hell!" she kept exclaiming. "So many people falling into hell! So many people in hell!"[30]

The doctrines of the Catholic Church become very clear when one has fought and suffered for them. Thomas Sennott, of Saint Benedict Center, is one who has had this privilege, and his lectures on the *Prophecy of Isaias* have brought home to us with what forcefulness God warned of the few who will be saved.

Isaias, the great prophet, who foretold so long before, the coming of Our Lord and the glorious establishing and perpetual flourishing of the Church of Christ, said the elect shall be as few as the forgotten ears of corn remaining on the stalks after the harvesting. Or as few as the bunches of grapes left on the vines after the pickers have finished their work. Or as few as the olives that remain after the shaking of the olive tree. Or as two or three berries on the top of a bough. (Isa. 17;5,6). And again:

Isa. 10;19: And they that remain of the trees of his forest shall be so few that they shall easily be numbered, and a child shall write them down.

The Cure d'Ars, a poor parish priest in France, who was canonized by Pope Pius XI, in 1925, used these texts from Isaias in his sermons over and over, in order to help his people to realize how few are saved. He used them not only as applying in the Old Testament, but in the New Testament as well, for all time. As a result, the Cure d'Ars won hundreds of souls to God. Penitents came to him from many countries, and toward the end of his life he was obliged to remain in the

---

[30] Despite the explicit teaching of Sacred Scripture and the constant teaching of the Church, the influential theologian Hans Urs von Balthasar denies that it can be known with certitude that anyone is condemned to Hell. His thoughts are presented in the book, *Dare We Hope "That All Men Be Saved"?* – Ignatius Press, 1986.

confessional almost all of the night and day.

Saint Francis Xavier gave up his family and his prestige at the University of Paris, to become the Apostle to the Indies. He said of the Indians, as he prayed for them: "Remember, Lord, how to Thy dishonor hell is being filled with these souls." Some priests, in our day, are beginning to drop this sentence of Saint Francis Xavier's from the Novena of Grace prayers. It was a Master of Novices, in a religious order, who first called Father Feeney's attention to the sudden omission, in the Novena of Grace pamphlets, of Saint Francis Xavier's clear-cut motive for going to the Indies to preach the word of God.

Saint Teresa of Avila said once that she saw, in a vision, souls falling into hell like snowflakes. "I think I would lay down a thousand lives to save even one of the men I saw being lost," she said.

The "golden-mouthed" Doctor of the Church, Saint John Chrysostom, writing about the salvation of bishops and priests said:

> I do not speak rashly, but as I feel and think. I do not think that many priests are saved, but that those who perish are far more numerous. The reason is that the office requires a great soul. For there are many things to make a priest swerve from rectitude, and he requires great vigilance on every side. Do you not perceive how many qualities a bishop must have that he may be apt to teach; patient towards the wicked, *firm and faithful in teaching the word*? How many difficulties herein.
>
> Moreover the loss of others is imputed to him. I need say no more. If but *one* dies without baptism, does it not entirely endanger his salvation? For the loss of one soul is so great an evil as no man can understand. If the salvation

of one soul is of such importance that, for its sake, the Son of God became man and suffered so much, think of the penalty the loss of one soul will entail. If he who kills a man in this life deserves death, how much more the others? Say not then to me: It was a priest or deacon who sinned. The faults of these are imputed to those who elected them....

If then one were to approach to the chief priesthood as an office full of solicitude and anxiety, no one would undertake it. On the contrary, nowadays, we aspire to this dignity as if it were a secular office, for the sake of glory and honour before men. What advantage will this honour bring?...

These words of Saint John Chrysostom are just as true in our time. We all know far more priests who are tepid, than priests who are afire for the glory of God. It is almost impossible in America today, as many have said, to point to one single Bishop and say, "There, without any doubt, is a truly holy man."

Saint Alphonsus Liguori, the founder of the Redemptorist Order, in his book *Preparation for Death*, writes that Our Lord said, of those who have given scandal and robbed Him of so many souls:

I will meet them as a bear that is robbed of her whelps. (Osee. 13;8)

Saint John Chrysostom said of the city of Antioch, with its hundred thousand inhabitants:

In our city, among so many thousands, scarcely can one hundred be found who will be saved, for in the youngsters is great wickedness, and in the elders deadness.

44   *Gate of Heaven*

Saint Augustine compared the Church to a threshing-floor, on which there is much more chaff than grain; more reprobate than elect; more damned than saved. As men lived, he said, so they die.

We know, then, from the words of Our Divine Lord and His Saints that even though Jesus died for all men, few—in comparison with all the inhabitants of the whole world—will dwell with Him in Heaven—by their own choice.

It need not have been so.

We commonly speak of an Archbishop's "receiving the red hat," when he is made a Cardinal. The red hat is the distinctive mark of a Cardinal. So also are the scarlet biretta and mantle which he wears. This is the dress of Cardinal Spellman, of New York. If Archbishop Cushing, of Boston, is made a Cardinal, red will be the color of his robes.

This color, red, for the robes of the princes of the Church, was most deliberately chosen. It was chosen because of the solemn privilege and duty which it signifies. The men who wear this color in their dress are reminded, by their garments, that they are to be ready and willing, at every moment, to shed their blood—their red blood—for the preservation and protection of the Faith.

To preserve inviolate the dogmas of the Catholic Church, and to be ready to die for them if necessary, is the duty of Cardinals, Archbishops and Bishops. If they do not preserve the Catholic Faith whole and entire for us, so that we may hand it down untouched to our children, they are not good shepherds. And they will, therefore, certainly go to hell when they die—and bring most of their flock with them.

Every priest and bishop is exempt from bearing arms. Priests are not, we are grateful to say, asked to shed their blood in battle. Our country leaves that to its soldiers. The blood of our bishops and priests is reserved for even a higher cause. It is to be shed for the word of Jesus Christ; for His truth. But it *is* to be shed for that, if necessary.

Now, our worry is not so much that Cardinal Spellman of New York, Archbishop Cushing of Boston, or Bishop Wright of Worcester, seems neither ready nor anxious to shed his blood for the Faith, sad as that is. Our worry is that what they are saying and doing makes of the Church such a pale thing, such a democratic thing, that no one will recognize it as the one true Church of Jesus Christ, or know that it is different in any way from other churches in the United States.

Our worry is that when they get through talking about the brotherhood of man in the Fatherhood of God—with no reference to Jesus Christ and His Mother, and all emphasis put upon the popular slogan "regardless of creed"—there will be no Catholic Church left for anyone, let alone themselves, to shed their blood for. And the number of the saved will be even less than it is today.

There is, in our time, a mistaken idea of the Mystical Body of Christ, and who comprise its members. Now, all men are not the *sons* of God. All men are the *creatures* of God. And a creature of God need not be a son of God.

Only those are sons of God who become so by adoption. Adoption is brought about—the adoption papers are passed, so to speak—by the reception of Baptism; and, as soon as possible, of the Holy Eucharist and the other Sacraments. We are, by these Sacraments, put into the state, the only state, in which it is possible for us to be elevated into the life of God. Baptism makes us sons of God. The Holy Eucharist nourishes, sustains, and maintains the Divine Life in us. We are at once sons of God, and children of Mary. We are by adoption—by grace—what Jesus is by nature.

No man is my brother who has not this incorporation in Jesus Christ. We may be members of the same human race, he and I, but we are not brothers. I am the adopted son of God and child of Mary. He is not.

And so our worry, therefore, is that we be mistaken, because of our Bishop's compromises and interfaith utterances, for the Old Testament dispensation, and not for the one true Church of Jesus Christ, of the New Testament. The Old Testament was the covenant of God the Father with man. The New Testament is the covenant of God the Son. What think ye of Jesus Christ? And of His Mother?

It has been said of our American Bishops that they seem to be seeking personal popularity among Protestants and Jews. This popularity many of them have achieved, as everyone knows. The tragedy, however, is that the price has been the lessening, compromising, and diluting of the Catholic Faith, for themselves and their people. Any priest would have but to go to Boston Common on Sunday afternoon and tell the truth there, as Father Feeney does; he would have but to go around from house to house, office to office, as the members of Saint Benedict Center do, to see at once in what an empty shell, in what a doctrineless waste, the Catholic Faith now resides.

While American Bishops are busy with men of other faiths, the basic doctrines which centrally protect the Catholic Faith are being denied and distorted. Catholics have not only been allowed, but have even been encouraged to hold their Faith so lightly that they believe practically everyone, without that Faith, can be saved. They say we have, of course, the comfort of the Sacraments and can congratulate ourselves on a stricter code of morals than those outside the Church, but in the end, it is all the same. Anyone who believes that he is going to heaven can do so, provided he sincerely holds—the error to which he is attached!

"But sincerity only makes it the more deplorable," you try to plead. "A man, reaching for a bottle of medicine, mistakes in the dim light the bottle of poison standing beside it for his medicine, and drinks from this wrong bottle. There is no question about his sincerity. He is just as dead as if he set out to drink the poison in the first place."

"I don't care what you say," is the answer we get to that. "You can't tell me! I know Protestants who are going to heaven ahead of Catholics."

"Do these Protestants receive the Body and Blood of Our Lord, in Holy Communion?"

"No, but they don't believe in It. They live beautiful lives. They never tell lies; they are scrupulously honest. They never talk about other people."

"They don't tell lies?"

"No."

"Isn't it a lie to say Our Lord is not truly present in the Holy Eucharist; that the Pope is not the Vicar of Christ; that Jesus was not speaking literally when he said: 'Except you eat the flesh of the Son of man, and drink his blood, you shall not have life in you'?"

"No. For them it is not a lie to say that. It would be a lie for us, but not for them. They do not believe it, that is all."

"You are talking about Revealed Truth!" we say desperately. "And there is no such thing as Revealed Truth being true for one, and false for another. If it is Revealed Truth, it must be true for everyone in the world. Anyone who interprets it in a way opposite to the way in which Jesus stated it, His Apostles and Evangelists recorded it in the Gospels, and the Catholic Church interpreted and preserved it for twenty centuries, is telling a lie."

"My friends are saying what they have been taught."

"They have been taught a lie, then. And it is up to them to discover it—which they will do, if they are really looking for the truth."

"My friends would die rather than tell a lie."

"In little things, yes. But in the big Thing that counts, they not only tell a lie, they live one. How can you say any life is truly beautiful—apart from the reception of the Body and Blood of Our Lord in Holy Communion?"

Catholics in our day seem to have lost all sense of the terrible sanctity of the Revealed Truth of God—of Truth with a capital *T*. They put Truth about the things of God in the same class as truths about the things of man—truth with a small *t*.

Anyone outside the Church who is never discovered in a lie about petty things, can always count on a reputation among Catholics as a saintly upholder of the truth. His whole life may be a denial of God's Word; he may in no way conform to God's Truth. This makes no difference. The Liberal Catholic will award him heaven because he has honesty in passing things.

The Church teaches that never is it right to tell a lie of any kind. But it distinguishes between lies which are venial sins, and lies which are mortal sins. Lies which are mortal sins, cut the soul off from the friendship of God, and leave it in mortal darkness. Should the person committing a mortal sin die without the remission of it, he would be damned for all eternity. This is not true of lies which are venial sins.

A lie can be at once the most trivial offense it is possible to commit against the law of God, and again the most heinous and blasphemous. To lie about the number of biscuits you had for breakfast, or the number of spoons of sugar in your coffee, is trivial enough. To lie about the number of Persons in the Blessed Trinity, or the number of natures in Jesus is a blasphemy against the truth of Revelation for which one will have to pay in terms of eternal damnation.

And that a Catholic could ever feel that refusal, on the part of anyone, to receive the Holy Eucharist could be compensated for by a scrupulous telling of the truth in little things, an honesty with regard to money, or a refraining from gossip, good though these things are in the moral order, is a blasphemy beyond description. Nothing in the whole world could compensate for the receiving of *one* Holy Communion. It is the difference between life and death.

The only Church which preserves the Holy Eucharist, with the safeguards Our Lord left for Its protection, is the Holy Catholic Church. Of this one true Church, Our Lord said, in the Holy Gospel, according to Saint Matthew (28;20):

> …Teaching them to observe all things whatsoever I have commanded you: and behold I am with you all days, even to the consummation of the world.

There can be but one Church, even as there can be but one Truth. No one denies that the Catholic Church is the one Church founded by Jesus Christ on Peter, the first Pope, and that it has come down, in the unbroken succession of Popes, straight from Saint Peter to Pius XII, in our day.

We do not say that all Catholics get to heaven. But we do say that they are on the right road to heaven, and that if they stay on this road, and observe its rules, they will surely get there. As Father Feeney often has explained:

> I do not say that being in the Catholic Church alone saves

you. I say that it is a condition without which you cannot be saved. If you just go over and stand on the road to New York, you won't get there. You have to go along the road. But, if you get on the wrong road to New York, it does not make any difference whether you go along it or stand on it. It is just the wrong road.

The Catholic Church is the Church in which Jesus Christ abides in the Holy Eucharist, the Sacrament of His Love. It is also the Church where, since she is never found apart from Him, Mary, God's Mother, is sure to dwell. Indeed, it is the place where every day she is loved and venerated.

Ignoring these ineffable Realities, Catholics in our day award heaven to Protestants and Jews for performances required even of any good Boy Scout. A Boy Scout must be pleasant, be thoughtful of others, be always smiling, never lose his temper, never say unkind words, never speak ill of another, must select his speech with careful precision. A polite sociologist recently made a fortune selling just such a code in more adult patterns in a book on how to make friends and influence people—not for the glory of God and love of Our Lord and His Mother, but for the speedy securing of personal popularity, prestige, power and money.

In the old days, when Catholics had the Faith, they recognized a saint as a man who, instead of wooing the world, disdained it; who, instead of accumulating money, gave it away; who, instead of fawning on and flattering the rich and powerful, excoriated and warned them; who, instead of seeking personal glory, shunned it. In our day, this ideal—which is no more than the following of Christ—is completely lost sight of.

"How can you talk this way?" a little Irish woman asked me. "Why can't you show more loyalty to the Church, and be quiet?"

"Loyalty to the Church means doing what we are doing," I tried to explain. "What you are asking is that we be loyal to bishops and priests who are preaching love of themselves and not love of Our Lord and Our Lady; who are weakening and watering down and losing the Faith for us all. It is cowardly to be politic and polite, cautious and not courageous in such a terrible time. Better to speak out now, in the hope of reaching some souls somewhere, than to wait until another war is upon us and an atom bomb blasts millions into hell. Someone has got to say that more are damned than saved, and *now* is the acceptable time! You should hear what Saint Anthony of Padua preached to the people about the priests and bishops of *his* time."

"Saint Anthony of Padua!" she answered, "that gentle little man? He's the humblest one of them all. I never think of him until I've lost something, and then he answers me right away; never holding it in for me that I forgot him in the meanwhile. He would not have the strong talk you have."

"You just listen to him!" I said. And I read to her some sermons of Saint Anthony.

Saint Anthony of Padua is known for having preached to the fishes, and as the heavenly finder of lost articles. For neither of these accomplishments was he made a Doctor of the Church, but for his learned and strong writings, and his still stronger sermons. These last, few people know about. Saint Anthony was called the "hammer of heretics." He preached to great numbers, sometimes as many as twenty or thirty thousand. Like all the saints, he was scathing in his denunciation of heresy, and sin, and weak leadership—even when he had openly to rebuke the hierarchy for their part.

Once Saint Anthony was invited to preach at a synod at Bourges, in France. There was a very well known prelate present, Archbishop Simon de Sully, who was a close friend of the King and the Pope. At the end of his sermon, Saint Anthony turned to the Archbishop, and said severely, "And now I shall speak to you, O Mitred One!" Before all the gathering, he accused and upbraided the Archbishop for his lack of the virtues necessary, and to be expected, in a leader of the Church. He converted him, and no one was more grateful than the Archbishop.

When abuses needed attacking, Saint Anthony did not know the meaning of fear. It never occurred to him to keep silent, or to make evasions. Famous preachers who listened to him—and who had not his love of God and His Mother or his singleness of purpose in serving Them—shivered at his boldness.

This is what Saint Anthony said, in a well-known sermon on Saints Peter and Paul:

> He is an idol (the priest neglectful of his flock), because he has hands for heaping up riches, but not for soothing the scars which remain from Christ's wounds. He has feet which he employs in going forth to better his housing and to demand his tribute, but not in taking him to speak God's Word. The praise of God is not heard from his lips. What is there in common between the Church of Christ and such a rotten image?...
>
> Thus the wolf, who is the devil, scatters the flock, and the thief, who is the heretic, makes off with it...Tell me, ye priests, is it in the prophets or in the Gospel, in the Epistles of Saint Paul or the Rules of Benedict and Saint Augustine, that you find these disputes, these lawsuits, these intrigues for transitory and perishable things?

"What do you think of that for strong language?" I asked my friend when I had finished reading to her this sermon of Saint Anthony's. "You never knew Saint Anthony was like *that*, did you?"

Her answer almost made me give up. "Oh," she said airily, "but he was a Saint, a long time ago."

In the fall of 1937, Father Leonard Feeney gave the Advent course of sermons in Saint Patrick's Cathedral, New York City, in the presence of Cardinal Hayes. One Sunday morning, before Father went into the pulpit, newspaper reporters approached him, and asked:

"What is to be the topic of your sermon today, and what is its message, Father?"

Father replied, "Boys, there is not one single thing I have to say in my sermon this morning that will even remotely interest you as newspaper reporters. I am going to talk about the necessity of Sanctifying Grace so as to get into the Kingdom of Heaven, and the means whereby it may be obtained. I have nothing to say on politics, or the European situation. I have no sociological message, or even an economic report on the nation. What you had better do is to say: 'Father Feeney preached this morning at Saint Patrick's Cathedral on Sanctifying Grace, and as far as we know, all went well.'"

This evidently intrigued the reporters, and, without Father Feeney's knowing it, they went around and sat in the congregation to listen to him preach. Spontaneously, in the midst of his sermon, Father said:

"Sanctifying Grace is given to each man, not merely to save him, but to make him a saint; to give him salvation in the fullest sense of 'Be ye perfect as your Heavenly Father is perfect.'

"And by the way," Father Feeney remarked, entirely

impromptu, "it is about time we had some saints in the United States. It is not because we cannot get Sanctifying Grace to make them. We hear lots about Saint Francis of Assisi, Saint Anthony of Padua, and Saint Therese of Lisieux. How about a Saint Barbara of Brooklyn, a Saint Helen of the Bronx, and Saint Robert of Jersey City?"

The newspapers next morning came out with the caption :

PRIEST WANTS AMERICAN SAINT
Suggests Saint Helen Of The Bronx
Saint Barbara Of Brooklyn

Time Magazine picked up the story. Saint Francis, Saint Knute, and Saint Joyce—for Father Francis P. Duffy, Chaplain of the Fighting 69th Regiment; Knute Rockne, the football coach of Notre Dame; and Joyce Kilmer, the poet who wrote "Trees"—were the first candidates who came to the mind of the *Time* reporter when an American saint was proposed.

"Far be it from me," Father Feeney said, "to deprecate Father Duffy as a kindly priest, Knute Rockne as a crack football coach, or Joyce Kilmer as a lovable poet, but they are about as far away from what I intended as I am, myself."

Father Feeney has, fourteen years later, lost his reputation as a preacher and a poet, a writer and a teacher. He has been defamed and calumniated, smeared and persecuted, because his defense of the doctrines of the Catholic Church was not pleasing to a politically-minded and timid hierarchy. He still feels that what the United States needs is an American saint. That is what he preaches, now more than ever, to the courageous men and women who have followed him into exile.

Catholics in the United States have been given, for

religious education, the *Baltimore Catechism*[31], and nothing else; not even the Bible. We have been left in ignorance, for the most part, of the Faith and its history. What we have gleaned from the Catechism about the doctrines, and from novena pamphlets about the saints, we seem to have sealed in a section of our minds, and labelled: *The Past*. That either the doctrines or the saints could still prevail in the twentieth century, Catholics for the most part refuse to consider.

When, like the horn of the Apocalypse, the Boston Heresy Case sounded the untaught doctrines of the Church on salvation out over the world, American Catholics were annoyed and shocked. The majority dismissed them, like examination questions:

No Salvation Outside the Catholic Church. *Answer*: Something the Church held for barbarians, if it held it at all. It has no possible reference to the saintly people we know as Protestants.

No Salvation without submission to the Pope. *Answer*: You could hardly ask that of people today, could you?

No Salvation without devotion to Mary. *Answer*: Shhhhhh! There's a place for everything, and everything in its place. Devotion is all right (for us), but Protestants and Jews would not understand. They would not like it. And we have to keep peace, so we can fight the Communists.

The Fathers and the Doctors of the Church. *Answer*: Never heard of them. Name one; I *might* know him.

The Saints. *Answer*: We need a different kind of saint today.

Few there are who are saved. *Answer*: I could not love a God who was not merciful. And I do not believe a merciful

---

[31] This catechism fell out of use after the Second Vatican Council, and was replaced by catechisms that are more liberal.

Gate of Heaven

God would send more people to hell than to heaven. If I have to believe that, and that there is no salvation outside the Church, in order to be a Catholic, then I guess I am just not a Catholic.

Comment: If the Church or our country feels that the kind of Catholic portrayed in this last answer will make a good fighter against Communism or any other threat, they are mistaken. At some point, such a person will be equally certain to say about his country: "Then I'm just not an American." Whoever has strong instincts for God, is bound to have strong instincts for everything else to which he owes service.

It has been God's way, both in the Old Testament and in the New, to punish not only the leaders, but the *people* as well, when weakness, laxity, and error crept into His fold. Because they had made to themselves gods of gold, God caused to be slain in one day twenty-three thousand Israelites. And the Gospel explains that:

Exod. 32;35: The Lord therefore struck the people for the guilt on occasion of the calf which Aaron had made.

The people are responsible for knowing the truth themselves, and of being aware when their shepherds are not teaching the full truth. Just as no man would deny when he is responsible for his own salvation, so also would he not deny that God has given him equipment enough for knowing when he has heard the truth and when he has not. God's grace is not lacking to anyone who will accept it, and the mind is made for truth, not for error.

Every Catholic knows, for instance, that when a Jewish rabbi, who denies the divinity of Christ, and a Protestant minister, who doubts it, get on a stage with a Catholic priest, who agrees to forget it for the evening (in the interests of mutual brotherhood), something is wrong. In the Catholic's heart of hearts he knows it.

When the leading voices extolling the national slogan: "regardless of creed" belong to our priests who every morning are heard in that other, and most sacred, cry—just before the Canon of the Mass:

> Sanctus, Sanctus, Sanctus Dominus Deus Sabaoth. Holy, holy, holy, Lord, God of Hosts. Heaven and earth are full of thy glory. Hosanna in the highest. Blessed is He Who cometh in the name of the Lord....

—every Catholic knows something is wrong.

And that knowledge makes *every* Catholic responsible. Christ, carrying His Cross, did not say to the women of Jerusalem when He met them, bewailing and lamenting Him: "Daughters of Jerusalem, weep for the high priest and the priests who have let this awful thing be done, and have despoiled you of your spiritual heritage." Rather, He said to them—who were apparently so innocent and grieving:

Luke 23;28: Daughters of Jerusalem, weep not over me; *but weep for yourselves, and for your children.*

There is only one bishop in the world who cannot make a mistake in doctrine; who cannot teach error. And that is the Bishop of Rome, the Holy Father. For us, that Bishop of Rome is Pope Pius XII.

The Bishop of Rome can make a mistake—*unless* he is speaking under certain conditions. These conditions are: (1) when he is speaking *"ex cathedra"* (from the Chair of Peter);

and (2) manifests his intention of defining a doctrine of faith and morals officially for the whole Church. At such a time, the Pope's teaching is *infallible*, that is, at such a time he is assisted, watched over, by the Holy Spirit so that he does not use his authority and his knowledge to mislead the Church. There actually have been times in the history of the Church when the Pope, speaking unthinkingly and from his first hasty judgment (and not *ex cathedra*), has erred in a matter of doctrine. Pope John XXII made just such a mistake once, and it was the people who discovered it, and called it to his attention. He investigated the matter, acknowledged his misconception, and corrected his statement. Father Mourret tells the story:

> Pope John XXII preached very often in Avignon churches. In the course of a sermon delivered on All Saints Day, he said that the souls of the blessed departed would not enjoy the full sight of God until after the general judgment. Although this opinion had been maintained by some of the Church Fathers, yet the general teaching of theologians was against it...The whole group of the "Spirituals" shouted "heresy!" The University of Paris was disturbed. Philip of Valois, king of France, and Louis of Bavaria, emperor of Germany, thought it proper to interfere, and, according to one chronicler, even to threaten. According to Villani, Philip of France threatened to inflict on the Pope the punishment reserved for heretics.
>
> Pope John at first could not restrain his anger, and went so far as to imprison a Dominican friar for contradicting his view. But, after gathering an assembly of cardinals and learned theologians, he gave up his opinion. Shortly afterwards, on his death-bed, he publicly retracted the doctrine he had uttered, *not as head of the Church, but*

simply as a private theologian. This great Pope lived after the manner of a simple monk, governing Christendom from a modest cell.[32] (Italics ours.)

It has sometimes shocked simple people to know that it is possible, even for the Pope when he is not speaking *ex cathedra*, to make a mistake in doctrine. However, that this should be so with regard to the Popes, seems to us more beautiful than otherwise. Jesus did not, in our Popes, promise us Vicars who were not human. The first Pope, Saint Peter, was the most attractively human of all the Apostles.

Peter's love was always betraying him into some humiliating situation. Seeing Jesus walking upon the sea, Peter, in his love, would have nothing but that he should go to meet Him, and show his enormous faith. Casting himself from the boat, he set out on foot across the water, became frightened, began to sink, and had to be caught up from under the waves by Jesus, to Whom he was crying out for help with all his might.

When the mob came out to seize Jesus, Peter struck the servant of the high priest and cut off his ear. Jesus told Peter to put his sword back into its scabbard, this was not the time for such action. And He healed the ear of the servant.

Peter protested that should the whole world be scandalized in Jesus, *he* never would deny Him. And he wore furrows into his cheeks from weeping, through all the rest of his life, for his three denials of Jesus on that very night of this avowal.

That Jesus should permit Peter, with his great, generous, impulsive heart, along with his boastful weakness, to be so portrayed for us in the Gospels—and at the same time to announce that it is upon this same Peter that He plans to build His Church—is at once the most touching evidence of trust in

---

[32] Mourret-Thompson, *A History of the Catholic Church.* Vol.5, p.91

Gate of Heaven

us and the most revealing credential of Emmanuel, God with us. No merely human ruler could afford such honesty, or such trust. Ballyhoo and pomp, settings for a superman, surround the presentation of worldly heads of government. Hitler or Mussolini could never have stood up under such an introduction as Peter's. Even the stammering presence of England's George VI is somehow covered up in the background of Queen Elizabeth's poise and the fanfare of slim young princesses.

The Catholic Church, with the simplicity and candor of Christ, explained, in the Vatican Council of 1870, that the Pope gains his knowledge just as any other man does. The Pope's knowledge, we are told, even when he is speaking infallibly, is not infused into him by God. Infallibility does not by any means do away with the necessity of study and learning. It simply, under certain conditions, guarantees that the conclusions drawn from study and learning are free from error. The Pope is guided by the Holy Spirit when he is *defining ex cathedra* so that he does not use his authority and his knowledge to mislead the Church.

The Pope , therefore, is infallible only when he is speaking *ex cathedra*. Bishops, Archbishops, and Cardinals are never individually infallible. They can, and often have, made mistakes in doctrine. The majority of the Bishops in England left the Catholic Church for Henry VIII's Church of England, at the time of the Protestant Reformation. The people of England were, among other names, called *Episcopalians*, precisely because they followed their Bishops—the Latin name for bishop being *episcopus*. Most of Germany became Protestant when its Bishops and priests followed Luther into heresy. Sweden and Denmark, Norway and Holland were lost in the same way.

The Catholics who followed their bishops and priests into heresy, in these countries, were punished by God. The people, as well as their leaders, were condemned. The Church tells us this when she teaches that we can have no hope for the eternal salvation of those who died heretics as a result of following their bishops and priests into Protestantism. The Church holds that this was misguided and sinful obedience. The people should have withstood the false doctrines. What is more, they should have admonished the heretical shepherds who were leading them astray.

How, it will be asked, could the *people* possibly know the truth under such circumstances, if their bishops and priests did not know it. The answer is that their bishops and priests did know it—just as they now know it—but they deliberately chose heresy over truth for many reasons. They chose it because (1) they were attached to their comfortable and rich livings, and did not want to give them up; or (2) because they were poor and wished to be rich, and this was one way to accomplish that; or (3) they wanted power, or prestige, or, what is sometimes even worse—popularity. And (4) in any and all events they did not truly love Jesus Christ and His holy Mother.

But how could the *people* know, even granted all this of their bishops and priests who went into heresy? How could the people, in a time of such confusion, know that they should not trust their shepherds? Surely doctrine is a territory in which their trust in their bishops is rightly established. Was it not beautiful and touching that they should obey? And is the Church not brutal to teach that we may not hope for the salvation, at least of the people who followed their leaders into heresy?

The answer is that even a child can tell when its parent is not telling the truth! God never leaves a soul without sufficient grace to recognize the truth, especially where its own everlasting salvation is concerned, and especially with regard to Eternal Truth. There was, in the experience of each one of us, a time when we calmly examined the teachings of our parents and teachers, and decided what portion of it was wise in our estimation, and what portion of it was not wise; in what way we would do things differently, if only in such simple matters as running a house.

It is the richness of wisdom in a parent's or teacher's instruction that a child is willing to receive, not the bare substantials of it. Every child knows when a parent is doing wrong, or a teacher is telling a lie. Let me see any father try to induce his child to believe that his drunkenness or wife-beating is praiseworthy, because it is parental example. Let me see any teacher tell a child that two and two are six, or that there are more moons than one in the sky, and hear how far the child can be led astray.

A priest who tells his parishioners, or a bishop who tells his subjects, how precious Jesus, Mary, Joseph, or the Blessed Eucharist are, or how august is the dignity of the Pope, will be believed; and will have the love and support of his listeners who are of good faith. But just as soon as a priest or a bishop tries to dispense with Jesus, Mary, Joseph, the Blessed Eucharist, or the Pope, even the dullest member of his congregation or his diocese knows that he is teaching heresy. There is a point beyond which the people cannot be deceived, even by those they are disposed to love and honor, as they are their bishops and priests.

Everybody in the Archdiocese of Boston, for example, knows, in his heart, that there is no quicker way to rub out Jesus, Mary, Joseph, the Blessed Eucharist, and the Pope, than to say that there *is* salvation outside the Catholic Church.

Neither Archbishop Cushing nor Bishop Wright—nor Cardinal Spellman—by evasive statements or scandalous silence, can for very long mislead true Catholics into thinking that this country is not thoroughly infected with heresy.

The following chapters of this book will show how the quickest way in the world to rub out the Blessed Sacrament, Our Lady, Saint Joseph, and the Holy Father is to say that there *is* salvation outside the one true Church instituted to preserve them. But even if no book were written, Catholics everywhere would still be responsible for knowing the truth and keeping the Faith.

Many times, in the history of the Church, the people have actually been the ones inspired by the Holy Spirit with regard to the true Catholic doctrine. For example, the Immaculate Conception of Our Blessed Lady was believed in the early centuries of the Church, although it was not defined. The writings of Saint Ephrem [33] alone prove this to be true. When, in later centuries, this doctrine came to be doubted, it was the people, and not the theologians, who affirmed Our Lady's Immaculate Conception. The people held processions in the streets, proclaiming it. It was their insistence that sent the theologians back, again and again, to examine the Holy Scriptures and the Tradition of the Church, until they at last discovered what the people all along had known, from their simple faith, and had never doubted.

When the Blessed Virgin Mary was called the Mother of Christ, but not the Mother of God, by Nestorius, the Patriarch of Constantinople, in 428, it was the people who immediately rose up in protest. They marched through the streets in torchlight processions, and angrily stormed the episcopal

---

[33] Saint Ephrem the Syrian is a Father and Doctor of the Church who died in 373.

residence, shouting: "We have, indeed, an emperor, but no bishop. We have no bishop!"

Our Lord says, in the Sermon on the Mount:

Matt.6;21: For where thy treasure is, there is thy heart also.

If the Faith is our treasure, and our heart is really in it, we will see that thieves do not break through nor steal it. We will guard it as our pearl of great price, which it is. And if we are not on guard at all times——as men are over worldly treasure—we will lose it. But we deserve to lose it, if we hold it so lightly, and we deserve to dwell, for that same reason, for all eternity in the depraved impoverishment of Hell.

There have been thieves of all kinds in history; thieves of all kinds in Holy Scripture. There was the "thief who came in the night"; the Samaritan who "fell among thieves." There was the bad thief, on the Cross beside Jesus. There was even the good thief, who stole heaven. But the worst thief of all time, for whom there is no honor even among thieves, was Judas. Judas was one of Christ's chosen twelve. Jesus chose him, not only to be one of His Catholic priests, but to be one of his Bishops, as were all the Apostles.

And Judas turned out to be a thief. He sold that which was not his—the life of Jesus. It is shocking that this could happen to a bishop in the highest consistory of all, that of the twelve Apostles. But it bears a moral for us: Let us watch out that other false bishops do not, like thieves in the night, snatch from us the eternal life of our souls.

Chapter III

If the Justice of God is as easy of appeasement as Catholic Liberals make it, *why was the price of man's Redemption so high?* It required the laying down the life of the Son of God to pay for it. Jesus Christ became Man, suffered, and died, to satisfy His Father for the sin of Adam's disobedience.

It is beyond man's power to realize the tremendousness of the cost of his Redemption. Trillions of dollars, or all the wealth of the world, could not approximate it. The very life of God, as we have said, in the nature He took from Mary, was needed to redeem us from *one* sin, in which we all had a part.

How Catholics today, in the light of this almost unrealizable fact, dare to teach that practically anyone can be saved, in any way he chooses to think out for himself, apart from the stern precepts of Christ, our Redeemer, we do not know. We have had two years at Saint Benedict Center in which to think over the enormity of this presumption on the part of Liberal Catholics, and it scares us more today than on the day it first officially was brought home to us, in the headlines of a newspaper, when we found ourselves interdicted for saying salvation could be found only in the one true Church of Jesus Christ.

The teaching of Liberal Catholics with regard to salvation, we have now come to see, can have but one explanation: these Catholics have, whether they realize it or not, lost their Faith. The Book of Wisdom teaches that when man has lost his Faith, he loses with it his fear of God; and a terrible presumption comes to take the place of his fear.

It is of such presumption that we have become most aware in Catholic writing since the Boston Heresy Case brought out the heretical ideas which have been under the surface of Liberal Catholic thought for over a hundred and fifty years. Fear of the Lord is the beginning of wisdom, and the end of wisdom is the end of fear of the Lord. A Catholic loses everything when he has lost his Faith. He becomes like a blind fool, rushing in where angels veil their faces. And lessons a child could see are—because of his perverse blindness—lost to him.

Surely the more than extraordinary cost of our Redemption should teach us that it is manifestly a monstrous thing for man to set his mind against the Will of his Creator. *And that it is difficult, and not easy, to get into heaven.*

Archbishop Cushing said recently: "I don't like all this talk about a narrow road. Most people, as I find them, are good. If I don't see you in heaven when I get there, I'll know it's because you haven't died yet."

This statement shocked even us, who have long grown used to the appalling lack of orthodoxy of our Archbishop. This avowal is in complete opposition to the teaching of Jesus Christ. Our Lord told us:

Matthew 7:13: Enter ye in at the narrow gate: for wide is the gate and broad is the way that leadeth to destruction: and many there are who go in thereat.

14: How narrow is the gate and strait is the way that leadeth to life: *and few there are that find it!*

The remainder of this discourse of Our Lord in the seventh chapter of Saint Matthew is of great significance also, since in it Jesus makes the people responsible for knowing whom to follow. He gives them rules by which they are to be guided.

Matthew 7;15: Beware of false prophets, who come to you

in the clothing of sheep, but inwardly they are ravening wolves.

I know it is hard to see a ravening wolf in an outwardly kindly face, but it is our obligation to do so, or else be swallowed up. Arius was a kindly priest. He was handsome, and he had most pleasing manners. He wrote popular songs, and won thousands of admirers in one way or another. But he deceived three-quarters of the Catholic world, patriarchs, bishops, priests, and people, and led them into the Arian heresy.

Matthew 7:18: A good tree cannot bring forth evil fruit: neither can an evil tree bring forth good fruit.
19: Every tree that bringeth not forth good fruit shall be cut down and shall be cast into the fire.
20: Wherefore by their fruits you shall know them.

In our day of Red Cross propaganda, Community Chest campaigns, Red Feather drives, it is difficult not to count as *good fruit* the collecting of huge sums of money by our Bishops, and the building by them of hospitals and homes. These are not, however, the fruits Jesus spoke of when He called his first Bishops:

Come ye after me, and I will make you to be *fishers of men.*

Jesus is hungry for souls, not for hospitals. There are many hospitals, but only one Church. It does not require an Archbishop to build a hospital, but it does require an Archbishop to preserve the Church. The Church began without money; it could get along without money. The monks of the

West built Christendom, after the fall of the Roman Empire, out of evangelical poverty. They gave up their money in order to do it. The only destitution that is absolutely tragic is the destitution of a world without the Faith. The good fruit by which a bishop is, in the end, known, is the quality of the Faith in his diocese.

A large turn-out of people for Church services, an intensive building program, a succession of pilgrimages, do not necessarily indicate a high quality of faith. All these things were present at the beginning of every period of decline in the Church. Godfrey Kurth writes of the Church just a few years before the catastrophe of the papal exile in Avignon:

> The First Jubilee was celebrated in Rome, in 1300, whilst Boniface VIII[34] occupied the chair of Peter. During the course of that year, the Pope, from the windows of his palace, saw a Christian world pass before him, going to the tombs of the Apostles in order to gain the indulgences of the Jubilee. The Eternal City then presented an incredible spectacle:—there were never fewer than two hundred thousand visitors, a truly astounding number if we consider the primitive modes of travel in those days. An eyewitness has described for us, in immortal verse, these vast throngs crossing the bridge of Saint Angelo on their way to and from the Vatican; those going held the right, those coming back the left, as is done at the present day on the bridges of the large German cities. Certainly in this year of boundless enthusiasm, when the Pope almost seemed to be more than a mere man and saw the whole

---

[34] Benedict Caetani, pope from 1294-1303.

of mankind at his feet, he needed an act of profound humility to resist the suggestions of such high fortune....

And indeed, thus passed the glory of this world for Boniface VIII. Before his death, this old man, at the age of seventy-seven, had to assist at the catastrophe which threatened to engulf the incomparable destinies of the Papacy. Two years after the triumph of the great Jubilee, the mercenaries of the Most Christian King seized the Vicar of Christ in his own palace, and the nation which called herself the eldest daughter of the Church attempted to crush the Roman See. The Pope, when on the brink of the grave, overwhelmed with sorrow and humiliation, knew that a dreadful revolution was consummated, or at least that its principle had been triumphantly affirmed, and that, for centuries to come, the rule of human society had been wrested from the Vicar of Jesus Christ.

Pope Pius XII last year looked out upon the Jubilee of the Holy Year of 1950. Many more hundreds of thousands pilgrimaged to the feet of Pope Pius XII, because of modern modes of travel, than set out across Europe on foot to Pope Boniface VIII in 1300.

Pope Pius XII is facing, however, just such a critical time, as did Pope Boniface VIII. In neither situation, Pope Boniface's or Pope Pius', was it the danger from without which brought on the catastrophe. France (the eldest daughter of the Church), under Philip the Fair, and Russia in our own day, under Stalin, both could have been overcome were the Church strong from within. But the glitter of liturgical performance is often mistaken for genuine fervor. The form has been known to remain after the matter is spent. A rosy red apple seldom warns of the worms within.

Father Feeney once in a poem said of liturgy without dogma:

> And, by the way,
> Speaking of how to pray,
> Dogmas come first, not liturgies.

Pope Boniface VIII met his crisis with all the glorious power, the holy wrath, the uncompromising courage of Saint Peter's successor. Before they murdered his body, the sword of his spirit flashed, and the divinely guided flame of it scorched and burned the evil heresy of his time.

The weapon which Pope Boniface VIII used in order to combat the foes of the Church is the most solemn and mighty force in the world. It is a weapon we pray Pope Pius XII will see fit to make use of in our tragic crisis. This weapon, this arresting force, is the word of God. With his back to the wall, fighting for the Church and his own life, Boniface VIII hurled at his enemies and the whole world the *infallible definition*, the magnificent exposition, the clear and unmistakable statement of pure Catholic doctrine contained in the bull, *Unam Sanctam*.

"Urged by faith," Pope Boniface stated in the *Unam Sanctam*, "We are obliged to believe and to hold that the Church is one, holy, catholic, and also apostolic. We firmly believe in her, and We confess absolutely that outside of her there is neither salvation nor the remission of sins..."

And then, to let the world know he was defining ex cathedra and that what he was declaring had always been a part of the Deposit of Faith—that is, had been taught by Jesus through the Apostles and been part of the Tradition of the Church—the Pope went on:

> Furthermore, We declare, say, define and pronounce, that it is wholly necessary *for the salvation of every human creature* to be subject to the Roman Pontiff.

It was after the release of this definition that the enemies of the Church decided once and for all to get rid of Pope Boniface VIII. They trapped him in a little Italian town, Anagni, as he was without defense. Seeing them coming, the venerable old Pope put on all his papal vestments and awaited them, holding in his hands the keys of Saint Peter.

Five days later Pope Boniface VIII was dead. But the Church was safe. Dante, in the *Purgatorio*, writes of Pope Boniface VIII:

> I see the *fleurs de lis* enter Anagni, I see Christ imprisoned in His Vicar, I see Him again given over to derision, I see Him again drenched with vinegar and gall, and crucified between new thieves.

It is a dangerous thing to say there is no salvation outside the Catholic Church, nor without personal submission to the Pope, nor without devotion and love for the Mother of God, but death is a sweet price for such a cause, and the servant is not above the Master.

In the beginning of the sixteenth century, just before the Church entered the greatest struggle of all (against Protestantism) there was no hint that the Faith was ready to be lost in wholesale fashion. Great numbers of churches were being erected, and richly adorned with art. Thousands upon thousands of pilgrims set out for the holy places; and gorgeous processions were seen in the streets of all the great cities of Europe. The splendor of the pomp and ceremony surrounding the Cardinals and Archbishops, as they took part in these processions, or even as they travelled with their retinues from place to place, bespoke a flourishing Church, popular, destined to go on so forever. However, as in our day, all this did not bespeak a holy hierarchy.

The Princes were great collectors of relics which the people, in large numbers, journeyed to venerate. Indulgences were prized, not something sheepishly acknowledged. I have always remembered Father Feeney's reply, at Saint Benedict Center, to a Harvard student's accusation: "But the Church sold indulgences!"

"Yes," Father said, "indulgences were sold, but that was at a time when people believed in indulgences, and felt that spiritual benefits were more valuable than material ones; indeed, they were willing to sacrifice money for the sake of spiritual values. Before I go on to being scandalized—which I am—at indulgences being sold, I want you, first, to be scandalized at the fact that no one could sell an indulgence to anyone now, if he wanted to, because there is no longer any Faith."

There were more books in the world than ever before, in the beginning of the sixteenth century. The printing press had then been invented fifty years. Editions of the Bible came off the new presses, translated into the various European languages.

The people loved to listen to sermons, and there were famous preachers to be had, whose eloquence moved the crowds. It was the day, too, of famous scholars. Rich merchants spent their money in the founding of schools and libraries. As the crown of his eminence, when a prince or an archbishop became rich and influential enough, he built a university, or added a college to an already well-known university. Cardinal Wolsey had a college at Oxford; Luther was the most popular professor in Frederick the Wise's new university, Wittenberg. Frederick was so proud of his university that he supported Luther as much out of loyalty to it as because he followed Luther's doctrine, at least in the beginning.

In spite of all these signs and conditions, scarcely twenty-five years after the opening of the century, the same people who flocked to services, made novenas, and venerated relics, left the Church—apostatized—in droves. They joined their bishops and priests, their princes and kings, in pillaging the churches, burning relics, confiscating monasteries. They fattened and grew wealthy on the possessions of the Church, and they martyred the good priests who were left, at their altars.

It will be wondered how such a complete reversal could take place, almost over night. But actually it did not happen almost over night. It had been a long time coming, and all the pomp and circumstance, all the outward show were but the brilliant trappings on a diseased and wounded body. That which would have preserved the vitality of the body had gone. It had been fed on sweets, and denied bread. The Church was satiated with liturgy, starved for doctrine.

There had been no strong doctrinal teaching for many years, before the Protestant Reformation. Superstition and ignorance had taken the place of knowledge, such as was to be had in the days of Saint Thomas Aquinas. Novenas, pilgrimages, superficial devotions can have a basis of superstition not possible when the Faith is on a good dogmatic foundation, and dogma had been scandalously neglected by the Renaissance Popes.

It is dogma which preserves the vitality of the Faith; dogma which is its staff of life. Every dogma must be kept faithfully. The loss of one means the loss of all. The Faith was all but mortally wounded, at the time of Luther. The Faith of Christendom, the Catholic Faith, was stricken, and all Europe with it, and the world is suffering now from this blight, which is still upon it.

I write in the middle of the twentieth century, over four hundred years after the Protestant revolution. It truly frightens me, as I sit here in Saint Benedict Center, punished by our Archbishop for devotion to dogma, to see all around me the same conditions which prevailed before the catastrophe of Luther. There is the same outpouring of apparently devout Catholics as at that time, the same devotion without dogma, the same blind following of worldly men. And the same dying Faith.

Boston is called a "Catholic City." Certainly, superficially viewed, it presents such a picture. Fifty thousand men march at dusk into Braves Field, a baseball stadium, in Boston, Massachusetts. They hold lighted candles in their hands, and recite the Rosary of the Blessed Virgin Mary. It is a beautiful sight, as darkness deepens.

Mechanics Building, on Huntington Avenue in Boston, an ugly, massive monstrosity, used in its long utilitarian history for anything and everything—a boxing match, a lumberman's exposition, a sports meet, a flower show—becomes the setting, under ecclesiastical arrangement, for the Holy Sacrifice of the Mass, with special liturgical emphasis. The Sacraments of Baptism and Confirmation are administered there.

Then, outgrowing even Mechanics Building, we move on,

not to our great cathedral, but to the Boston Garden, of new and fabulous proportions, and Caesar-like setting. Hollywood comes to us there, at the invitation of our Archbishop, and Broadway, too. Vast sums of money are made by him, in the Boston Garden, for charity, which we are told will be used for the care of men's bodies. The charity which feeds men's souls, and which can be dispensed inexpensively from a pulpit or a highway and a byway, seems not to lend itself to publicity, and, besides, would not be savored by heretics and infidels, whom we must in no way disturb, not even to give them eternal salvation.

We have had processions in the streets of Boston, too, only we called them parades. It took over nine hours for the pageantry of one such parade to pass the reviewing stands. Our Archbishop joined the marchers several times, and the newspapers were full of pictures of his colorful figure, in its beautiful robes, his subjects kneeling before him in the streets to kiss his ring and receive his blessing. His auxiliary Bishop was beside him, with a look in his eyes not unlike that of ambitious young bishops in the retinues of high churchmen in the early sixteenth century.

In the light of Pope Boniface's experience and that of the sixteenth century world, it does not surprise us to know that it was out of all this Catholic activity, all this outward show of a flourishing Church, that there was made evident, one day, the same unmistakable symptom of the same deadly disease within the body of the Church as had caused the disaster of the Reformation. The root of the disease was exactly the same: negligence and ignorance of dogma.

The most basic doctrines of the Catholic Church on salvation were denied by the Rev. William L. Keleher, S.J., President of Boston College. He made this denial when he explained to the Boston newspapers why he had fired three members of the College faculty for holding and teaching the doctrines. Archbishop Richard J. Cushing and Bishop John J. Wright, his auxiliary, supported the denial (which immediately received world-wide publicity) by refusing to affirm the doctrines, by keeping silent on the subject of them, and by silencing Father Leonard Feeney and interdicting Saint Benedict Center, the Catholics who held the doctrines and taught them.

The weak condition of the Church in Boston, in spite of the religious display that surrounds it, was revealed in the handling of the Boston Heresy Case. The defined doctrines denied in this "controversy" (why there should be a controversy about doctrines held for centuries without question, and defined many times in the settlement of other questions, we never have been able to understand) were, as millions now know: there is no salvation outside the one true Church of Jesus Christ nor without personal submission to the Pope; nor without love and devotion to the Mother of God.

Matthew 7;17: Even so every good tree bringeth forth good fruit; and the evil tree bringeth forth evil fruit.

20: Wherefore by their fruits you shall know them.

"Outside the Catholic Church there is no salvation," is not only a dogma many times defined, as we say in Chapter I, but it is, as we have said, one of the most basic of all doctrines. To teach the opposite would lead eventually to the denial of every single dogma of the Faith. Saint Augustine says, and the history of the Church proves, that to deny one doctrine, is to deny all. And such denial on the part of a bishop can in no way be considered anything but the most evil of *evil fruits.*

Denial of dogma is, in fact, heresy, and one denies dogma just as much by not defending it and not affirming it when it is questioned, as by outright repudiation.

Our Lord tells us, in the seventh chapter of Saint Matthew, what He will say and do to a servant whose works (or fruits) are evil. Furthermore, He places responsibility on *us* for recognizing such a servant. Otherwise, we will merit the same punishment. Our Lord says:

Matthew 7:21: Not every one that saith to me, Lord, Lord, shall enter into the kingdom of heaven: but he that doth the will of my father who is in heaven, he shall enter into the kingdom of heaven.

22: Many will say to me in that day: Lord, Lord, have not we prophesied in thy name and cast out devils in thy name and done many miracles in thy name?

23: And then I will profess unto them: I never knew you. Depart from me, you that work iniquity.

24: Every one therefore that heareth these my words and doth them shall be likened to a wise man that built his house upon a rock.

25: And the rain fell and the floods came and the winds blew and they beat upon the house, and it fell not, for it was founded on a rock.

26: And every one that heareth these my words and doth them not shall be like a foolish man that built his house upon the sand.

27: And the rain fell and the floods came and the winds blew: and they beat upon the house. And it fell: and great was the fall thereof.

28: And it came to pass when Jesus had fully ended these words, the people were in admiration of his doctrine.

Gate of Heaven

Hospitals and homes and buildings, pomp and popularity, fall before the floods, the winds, and the rain. They can be built up again, and nothing very much has been lost or gained. Building projects have come and gone since Adam, our common father, one dark day found himself in need of shelter. Another ancestor, Noah, outlived our life-span nine times, with never, as far as we know, the benefits of hospitalization. The rock upon which the wise man built, in Saint Matthew's Gospel, foundationed no temporal abode. The wise man built for his eternal home—upon the rock of Peter, the Catholic Church.

Building achievements do not determine the stature of a bishop. One bishop, Pope Saint Celestine,[35] neither possessed anything nor built anything. He ran away from his simple apartment in the Vatican, back to his solitary cell. He was unpopular. Dante was so angry with him for running away from the Papacy, depriving the Church of a saintly Pope, that he placed him in the *Inferno*. (It must be said for Dante that he did not take his work half so seriously as do his admirers of our day. Pope Celestine was canonized during the lifetime of Dante, and the poet, a true Catholic, knew Pope Celestine then infallibly to be in heaven. Yet he did not turn around and put him in heaven in the *Divine Comedy*. He left him in hell, where he is not.)

A good or bad bishop is known, not by his building program or the amount of money he has in the bank as a "corporation sole," with the power to command those below him to surrender funds to him under pain of canonical disobedience. He is not known even by personal popularity. A good bishop is known by whether or not he has kept the Faith,

---

[35] Pope Celestine V, Peter of Morone or Saint Peter Celestine who died in 1296.

for himself and for his subjects.

And the Catholic Faith is preserved by literal adherence to its doctrines, not by compromise of them.

"Regardless of race, color, or CREED," the popular slogan, is the exact opposite of the defined doctrine, "Outside the Catholic Church there is no salvation." Father Feeney has carefully explained on Boston Common on many Sunday afternoons: "The priest's greatest gift to his children is the Body, Blood, Soul and Divinity of Our Lord and Savior, Jesus Christ, which he holds in his hand under the appearance of bread. Any race and any color may receive this gift, and it is the same Christ in every Communion. Once you have the Holy Eucharist in your hand as a priest, you need no longer think of race and color. But if you do not think of creed when you have this Bread in your hand, it will be useless to call it the Bread of Life."

Narrow is the gate, and strait is the way. And the people are as responsible as their leaders. They have their Faith and its Sacraments, and therefore light by which their eyes may see and their ears hear and they may know when they are being led astray, and other than the truth is being preached to them.

When Fakhri Maluf[36], on a long trip from Saint Benedict Center, called upon His Excellency, Archbishop Cicognani, the Apostolic Delegate[37]—after the Boston Heresy Case first appeared in the newspapers—the Archbishop's secretary told him that matters of conscience with regard to dogma were of such major importance that any Catholic in the world was allowed the privilege of appealing directly to the Holy Father on the subject, and was not obliged to go through the ordinary

---

[36] He later became Br. Francis, M.I.C.M.

[37] He served in that position from 1933-58.

channels. It is true that Saint Benedict Center appealed many times, both to the Apostolic Delegate and to Rome, and received no answer, but we are consoled by the fact that our Holy Church has made it possible for us to know the truth and hold it, until the day His Holiness, the Pope, once more affirms the previous infallible pronouncements on salvation. We know, too, by the same Catholic Faith, that any new pronouncement can in no way differ from the old.

In the meantime, we did have one slight encouragement of which there can be no doubt. In the midst of his encyclical on other matters, Pope Pius XII, in the summer of 1950, took time in the *Humani Generis*, to make the declaration already quoted in the second chapter of this book:

> Some reduce to a meaningless formula the necessity of belonging to the True Church in order to gain salvation.

With this comfort, we can go on, praying each day to the great Mediatrix of All Graces for courage to maintain our glorious Faith, no matter how alone we may seem to be, no matter how persecuted, knowing, if we do maintain it, that the voice of Jesus will never say to us that which we could not bear:

"I never knew you."

Chapter IV

It seems to us that when something is done about Liberal Catholicism in the United States, it will be the common sense of the simple Catholic people which will bring it about. A return to the pure Catholic Faith brought from Europe by our grandparents and great-grandparents will never be achieved out of the terrible confusion into which the American theologians have plunged themselves. Such a welter of words, signifying nothing, which has come out of efforts to explain away the Pope's simple statement in his encyclical, *Humani Generis*, on no salvation outside the Church, we have never before seen.

It is with relief that we have turned from the crazy logic of these articles to the shrewd wisdom of men who have come to us from Boston Common.

"In the name of God, Father," they say to Father Feeney, "what has happened to our priests?"

One of our most steadfast friends came to see us, with an Irish catechism in his hand.

"This is Butler's Catechism, Father," he said, "and many's the time I was belted across the palms of my hands for not knowing it. The very thing they're persecuting you for now, I had to learn over and over again when I was a boy. Let me read it to you. If you want, I'll send for some more of these for you. Now, listen:

"Here, in the Most Rev. Dr. James Butler's Catechism, which was reprinted in 1950, on page 26, it says:

2. *Question*: How do you call the true Church?

Answer: The Holy Catholic Church.

3. *Q.* Is there any other true Church besides the Holy Catholic Church?

No; as there is but *one Lord, one Faith, one Baptism, one God, and Father of all,* there is but one true Church. (Ephes. iv. 5,6.)

4. *Q.* Are all obliged to be of the true Church?

A. Yes; no one can be saved out of it. (Acts,ii; John x; Matt. xxviii.)

5. *Q.* Will strict honesty to every one, and moral good works, insure salvation, whatever Church or religion one professes?

A. No; unless such good works be enlivened by *faith, that worketh by charity.* (Gal.v,6.)

6. *Q.* Why must our good works be enlivened by faith?

A. Because the scripture says, *without faith it is impossible to please God; and he that believeth not shall be condemned.* (Heb. xi, 6; Mark xvi, 16.)

8. *Q.* Must our good works be also enlivened by charity?

Yes; for Saint Paul says, *If I should distribute all my goods to feed the poor, and if I should deliver my body to be burned, and have not charity, it profiteth me nothing.* (I Cor. xiii, 3.)

Q. What is that charity of which Saint Paul speaks?

A. That pure and sincere love of God, which make us do his will in all things, and be obedient to his Church, *which he commands us to hear.* (Matt. xviii, 17; Luke x, 16.)

10. *Q.* Which are the marks or signs of the true Church?

A. The true Church is one, holy, Catholic and Apostolical.

11. *Q.* How is the Church one?

A. In being *one body, and one fold*, animated by *one spirit*, under *one head, and one shepherd, Jesus Christ, who is over all the Church.* (Eph. iv, 4.)

12. *Q.* In what else is the Church one?

A. In all its members believing the same truths, having the same sacraments and sacrifice, and being under one visible head on earth.

"Take that last answer alone, Father," our friend said. "That makes sense to me."

The Italians and the French who have talked with us about the doctrine of no salvation outside the Catholic Church have, almost to a man, said that never in their countries, as children, were they ever taught anything else. The Italians refused to believe there could be a difficulty about the doctrine. They said our interdict must have been given us for some other reason. However, when they had discussed the dogma with their American parish priests, they realized what we were saying was true. They threw up their hands and told us that Father Feeney would have a hard time, and had better go straight to Rome to see the Pope about it. We convinced them that if we were unable to see Archbishop Cicognani, the Pope's delegate in America, we had very little hope of getting to His Holiness, even if we were able to go to Rome.

We have been sustained in our work by the warmth and love of many beautiful Italian Catholics.

The Catholic Church has never ceased to teach the doctrines of Christ and His Apostles. It will never cease to do so. Somewhere, the pure Catholic Faith will always be preached.

It is not true that there are many different ways of reaching God through religion. It is not possible for a sincere Protestant and a sincere Jew to get to heaven, unaided by the grace of the Sacraments, or without having offered, with the priest, worthy

Gate of Heaven

sacrifice, the Holy Sacrifice of the Mass, to God. It is not possible for anyone, furthermore, to attain heaven without having acknowledged and loved God's Mother, the Blessed Virgin Mary.

And it is not necessary, in order to know this, to have read books in theology. The Catholic Faith is at once so simple and so profound that a child can understand it, on the one hand, and scholars never exhaust it, on the other. Our Lord said, "Unless you be converted, and become as little children, you shall not enter into the kingdom of heaven." (Matt. 18;3.)

When a child arrives at the age of seven or thereabouts, he has attained the use of reason, and he is permitted to go to Confession and make his First Communion. At that age, he is able to understand the simple truths of his Faith. He knows, and is delighted in the knowledge, that Jesus became man and died to redeem him from his sins, and open heaven to him again. He knows that Mary is the gate of heaven, because she was the gate through which Jesus came on earth.

A child can understand that before Jesus went back to his Father in heaven He founded a Church, which is the only Church in which men can be saved. It is as simple as A B C to a child that if anyone were to found a Church, it would have to be God, and not man. And God would found only one Church, because if He founded more than one, it would mean that something was wrong with the first one—a child would reason—and God could never make a thing that had something wrong with it. It would have to be the best that could be, or else God would never make it. The Church could have bad men in it, but that would be men's fault, and not the Church's, and some day God would take the bad men away.

It would be clear to a child that anyone who was stubborn and proud and wicked enough to stay outside Jesus' Church would have to be punished. Punishment is a just thing, a child early discovers. One who did not love Our Lady and the Holy Father would be punished too, the child would add by way of postscript.

Now, no matter how old we grow, or how adult we become in other territories, religiously we have but to listen as children to the words of Our Lord speaking through the Apostles—and through his Church in its Saints and Doctors and Popes—to know that salvation was never promised to those outside the fold. If we hold to the simplicity of children in this all-important matter, the confused adultisms of intellectuals in the Church will not deceive us, or drag us into heresy.

Simply, then, from the words of Our Lord Himself, let us consider the case of the non-Catholic with regard to salvation.

First, we will take the case of the *Jew*. His case happens to be the most simple. There is no question at all about whose case is the most tragic—the Jew's, the Protestant's, the Mohammedan's, the Hindu's—for all are equally tragic. None of them can attain the Beatific Vision of God. God has said so. It does not matter how close they come, or how far away they are. To miss heaven at all is to miss it completely. And it is an unfathomable loss.

The Jew is unbaptized. Our Lord's words on those who are unbaptized are terribly clear. Jesus told us:

Mark 16;16: He that believeth and is baptized shall be saved: but he that believeth not shall be condemned.

John 3;5: Jesus answered: Amen, amen, I say to thee, unless a man be born again of water and the Holy Ghost, he cannot enter into the kingdom of God.

Even if we did not know that for almost two thousand

years the Jews, whom Jesus called a "stiff-necked people," have stubbornly and sinfully refused to acknowledge Him as the Son of God and the Messiah promised from the creation of the world, these words of Our Lord concerning the necessity of Baptism would be sufficient to tell us that they cannot enter into the kingdom of heaven—as Jews.

Someone has said that the Jews are like people waiting in a railroad station for a train that passed two thousand years ago.

And so we know that the Jews—unless before they die they come into the Catholic Church—cannot be saved *because Jesus said so.*

Second, we have the case of the *Protestant.*

A Protestant may or may not be baptized. If the Protestant's Baptism is valid, it suffices for admission into the kingdom of heaven only until the second requirement comes due. The second requirement is the receiving—when he reaches the use of reason—of two other Sacraments: Penance and Holy Eucharist.

And these two Sacraments a Protestant does not have in his church because (a) they are not believed in, or (b) they are unavailable in Protestant churches.

If, by some chance, the Sacraments of Penance and Holy Eucharist were believed in, Protestant ministers are without valid Holy Orders by which to confer them. The members of a Protestant congregation, therefore, are without Confession and without the Blessed Sacrament, which is the Body, Blood, Soul and Divinity of Our Lord and Saviour Jesus Christ, under the appearances of bread and wine.

Several Anglican ministers (of what is generally known as the Anglican Church in England and the High Episcopalian Church in America), knowing their Holy Orders are not valid, have, in recent years, fraudulently obtained true Holy Orders by going to Greek bishops for ordination. These ministers then administer the Sacraments, but they do so against the will of Jesus, and apart from the unity of the true Church. By administering the Sacraments of the Church with fraudulently obtained Holy Orders, such ministers are guilty of the Body and Blood of Jesus Christ, and every administration of the Sacraments by them is a sacrilege.

We see immediately the foremost reason why Protestants cannot be saved—because they do not receive the Blessed Sacrament. Our Lord was thunderingly direct, simple, and unmistakably clear on the eating of the Holy Eucharist for salvation. He said:

John 6;48: I am the bread of life.

49: Your fathers did eat manna in the desert, and are dead.

50: This is the bread which cometh down from heaven; that if any man eat of it, he may not die.

51: I am the living bread which came down from heaven.

52: If any man eat of this bread, he shall live forever; and the bread that I will give, is my flesh, for the life of the world.

53: The Jews therefore strove among themselves, saying: How can this man give us his flesh to eat?

54: Then Jesus said to them: Amen, amen, I say unto you: Except you eat the flesh of the Son of man, and drink his blood, you shall not have life in you.

55: He that eateth my flesh, and drinketh my blood, hath everlasting life: and I will raise him up in the last day.

56: For my flesh is meat indeed: and my blood is drink indeed.

57: He that eateth my flesh, and drinketh my blood, abideth in me, and I in him.

58: As the living Father hath sent me, and I live by the Father: so he that eateth me, the same also shall live by me.

59: This is the bread that came down from heaven. Not as your fathers did eat manna, and are dead. He that eateth this bread, shall life for ever.

60: These things he said, teaching in the synagogue, in Capharnaum.

But suppose the Protestants do not know the Holy Eucharist is God? the Liberal Catholics ask. Just imagine, we answer, the Real Presence of the Body, Blood, Soul and Divinity of Our Lord and Saviour, Jesus Christ, to be a fact, and God not to have made it easy for all of good will to find it! Just imagine God not to have provided a sacrosanct and singular citadel to preserve this Blessed Sacrament as God's great Gift to man! And just imagine any one of the Protestant churches being that citadel! Imagine what care any of the Protestant churches would take of the Precious Body and Blood of Jesus. Every single Protestant church did away with the Holy Sacrifice of the Mass and the Real Presence of Jesus Christ in the Holy Eucharist. The Anglicans, after depriving their people of the Holy Eucharist for over three hundred years, tried to bring It back—without valid Holy Orders by which to do so.

One of Father Feeney's tenderest stories is the experience of an Anglican nun, who was superior of an Anglican convent in Boston. Her nuns professed to believe in the Blessed Sacrament. They received "the Blessed Sacrament" from the hands of a priest who did not have valid Holy Orders. Now, one day the Anglican Bishop of Boston came to pay the Community an episcopal visit. This Bishop did not believe in the Holy Eucharist, at all, and so one of the nuns, for fear of offending him, took the "Blessed Sacrament" out of the tabernacle and hid it until the Bishop departed.

Whereupon, the Superior of the convent, knowing now for sure that the faith of her sisters was spurious, went upstairs and took off her habit. She resigned from the convent and from the Anglican Church. She became a humble Catholic laywoman, and lived on for many years in relative poverty—in comparison with the liturgical luxury she once enjoyed—secure in possession truly of the Real Presence of her Lord and Saviour in the Blessed Sacrament of His altar. She was Miss Julia Pember, and not only was she Father Feeney's friend,—I also had the privilege of having her for mine. And I know it shocked her when Catholics, themselves not realizing the Gift of God, would compliment her extravagantly for doing what she ought to have done, and for feeling no cost too much to pay for the pearl of great price, her Catholic Faith.

To put it, then, in simple, conversational terms: Imagine the Blessed Sacrament without the Pope to protect Its sacrosanct value, and imagine the whole world not being intended by God to take advantage of Its sacred familiarity!

Only one-sixth of the world is Catholic at the present time.[38] What sort of brutality could have entered the thought of our Church to induce its priests to keep its best gifts for itself, and hand out only religious rhetoric to the starving, hungering people of the world—whether their hunger be for food, which Jesus, in the Blessed sacrament, can satisfy; or for love, which the Spouse of the Holy Spirit—Our Lady—can appease.

The thing that happens when there is double talk as to where salvation is to be found by any arrangement other than the Rock upon which Christ built his Church, is that Jesus and Mary are made secondary values in the human salvation God

[38] The percentage of the Catholic world is closer to 20% at present.

Gate of Heaven

planned for man. And some proud, inhuman, diabolical substitute is given in place of the Word Made Flesh, Who dwells amongst us.

Either Mary the Mother of God is meant to be the Queen of every man's and woman's heart, or else there is no Blessed Virgin Mary. Either the Blessed Eucharist, the Body, Blood, Soul and Divinity of Our Lord and Saviour, Jesus Christ, in simple and innocent form is meant to be put into the mouth of every human being in this world by Christ's commandment, or else there is no such thing as the Presence of the Body, Blood, Soul and Divinity of Jesus Christ under the species of bread and wine.

Either Christ's legacy to man at the Last Supper, His last will and testament, His *magnum donum*, His greatest gift, is meant to be the Food apart from which there can be no salvation—or else it is not the Bread of Life. It is just one among many other nourishments, not one of them divine. And any church which has charge of the Blessed Eucharist—to keep it in divine protection—either tells the world that outside this church there is no salvation, or else it is not the church established by Christ,

Thanks be to God, the Father, Son, and Holy Ghost, and thanks be to the Blessed Virgin Mary, Mediatrix of All Graces, the Popes of the Roman Catholic Church, in clear definition, have told the world where salvation is to be found. These definitions I have given in an earlier chapter.

To sum it up, then, we have seen that there are those *who do not receive the Body and Blood of Jesus Christ* in Holy Communion. And these cannot have eternal life with God. These are the heretics and infidels.

Then there are those *who do receive the Body and Blood*

of Our Lord. These who do receive It, can receive It in three ways:

1)Unworthily; in the Greek Orthodox Church, or in an Anglican Church where a minister has surreptitiously obtained Holy Orders from a Greek Orthodox bishop. Those who receive It from such a priest are guilty of the Body and Blood of Jesus Christ.

2)There are those who receive It in the Catholic Church, and who think It is not necessary for salvation for those outside the Church. These do not really believe the Blessed Sacrament is the Bread of Life; and they, too, are guilty of the Body and Blood of Jesus.

3)And finally, there are those who receive It, and believe It is the Bread of Life both for themselves and for all mankind. These both love the Body and Blood of Jesus in Itself, and love the whole world, for whom It was intended.

John 6;40: And this is the will of my Father that sent me: that everyone who seeth the Son, and believeth in him, may have life everlasting, and I will raise him up in the last day.

And how shall every man have life everlasting?

John 6;55: He that eateth my flesh, and drinketh my blood, hath everlasting life: and I will raise him up in the last day.

Jesus could not tell us more clearly. The whole story of salvation is written in Holy Scripture, provided we read it with eyes that see. Jesus goes on, in this same chapter of Saint John, to give us an example of what happens when men refuse His flesh to eat, and His blood to drink. Saint John recounts:

John 6;61: Many therefore of his disciples, hearing it, said:

This saying is hard, and who can hear it?

62: But Jesus, knowing in himself that his disciples murmured at this, said to them: Doth this scandalize you?...

67: After this, many of his disciples went back: and walked no more with him.

It is difficult to portray the degree of privation, the depths of loss in this last sentence. To walk no more with Jesus is no more to be in His company. And before such bleak desolation words abandon me, for it is the very essence of hell—to be no more or ever in the company of God.

These disciples who walked away from Jesus were men He had loved. They had given up a great deal to follow Him. Jesus knew that what He had just said to them *was* a hard saying, for the drinking of blood was a forbidden and a heinous thing for a Jew. Too, this discourse on the Holy Eucharist was made by Our Lord about a year before the Last Supper—at which He instituted the Blessed Sacrament—and even the chosen twelve were still in need of many graces—let alone the disciples.

But *who* shall question God? And who presume to tell God what is merciful and what is not merciful; what is just and what is not just?

Isa. 40;13: Who hath forwarded the spirit of the Lord? Or who hath been his counsellor, and hath taught him?

Wisd. 9;13: For who among men is he that can know the counsel of God? or who can think what the will of God is?

14: For the thoughts of mortal men are fearful, and our counsels uncertain.

15: For the corruptible body is a load upon the soul, and the earthly habitation presseth down the mind that museth upon many things.

16: And hardly do we guess aright at things that are upon earth: and with labour do we find the things that are before us. But the things that are in heaven, who shall search out?

17: And who shall know thy thought, except thou give wisdom, and send thy Holy Spirit from above:

18: And so the ways of them that are upon earth may be corrected, and men may learn the things that please thee?

The history of the Chosen People is filled with instances of punishment for those who dared to question the word of God. Catholics in our day rarely read the Old Testament. They should do so, if only to have restored to them the *fear of God*. Fear of God is a salutary, just and holy thing. It is well to reflect—in our soft age—on the strong punishment God has meted out to those who offended Him.

Our first parents were banished forever from the Garden of Eden and condemned to work out their days by the sweat of their brow because they disobeyed one command of God.

"Look not back!" the angels of the Lord said to Lot and his wife, as they led them from the wicked cities of Sodom and Gomorrha. And because Lot's wife did not heed the order, because she decided for herself what she would obey and what she would not obey, she turned around and looked back—and was then and there turned into a pillar of salt. She became a horrible example for generations of her people—and for us.

God said to Moses, in Egypt:

Exod. 12;12: And I will pass through the land of Egypt that night, and will kill every firstborn in the land of Egypt both man and beast: and against all the gods of Egypt I will execute judgments: I am the Lord.

Gate of Heaven

This killing is, undoubtedly, shocking to the Liberals of our day, who in their dead faith and pious sentimentality, cannot bear the thought of God's refusal of heaven, in the New Testament, to those who reject His Sacraments, His Holy Sacrifice, and His Mother. But so contrary to the Liberal's standard is God's judgment of the just slaughter of the Egyptians, that He made a commandment upon the Jews to keep the day as a memorial:

Exod. 12;13: And the blood shall be unto you for a sign in the houses where you shall be: and I shall see the blood, and shall pass over you: and the plague shall not be upon you to destroy you, when I shall strike the land of Egypt.
14: And this day shall be for a memorial to you: and you shall keep it a feast to the Lord in your generations with an everlasting observance.

Even the faithful and holy Moses failed of the reward of his long years of striving—because one day he dared to *hesitate* before the word of God! On account of this, another, and not he, was appointed to lead his people into the Promised Land. Moses saw the Promised Land, but was not suffered to go into it.

On and on we might go. Over and over, it was necessary for God to punish men when they presumed to question His word. The destruction of Jerusalem, foretold by Our Lord in Saint Matthew and Saint Luke, when there should be a "tribulation such as hath not been from the beginning of the world until now, neither shall be," (Matt. 24;21) was a punishment so terrible that historians have been at a loss to describe it. It occurred in the year 70 A.D., about thirty-seven years after the beginning of the Church. A million people perished during the siege of the City which had witnessed the Passion and Death of the Son of God and in whose streets Saint James the Apostle (the cousin of Jesus who so strikingly resembled Him in appearance) was stoned to death.

When God speaks, we, His creatures, must listen and assent; or take the consequences.

Isa. 66;2: My hand made all these things, and all these things were made, saith the Lord. But to whom shall I have respect, but to him that is poor and little, and of a contrite spirit, *and that trembleth at my words.*

Jesus Christ, Who is God, has spoken on the subject of salvation. His words have been reiterated down the centuries by His Church, in infallible pronouncements. It were well for us to heed them.

Chapter V

The doctrine of No Salvation Outside the Catholic Church is a *hard saying* for a great many people today. There is one question with regard to it which practically everybody puts to us.

"What about the poor native on a desert island?" Or, "What about the native in the middle of Africa? Is it fair for God to send him to hell when he has never heard of the Catholic Church?"

We are often tempted to reply, "Your worry about a hypothetical native is odd, in view of the salvation problems staring at you in members of your family and your neighbors next door. But since you will not settle down to think about the matter at home until the apparent plight of the native is settled, let us consider the native."

Most people seem to think that Our Lord and Saviour Jesus Christ, Who is the Infinite God, never thought of or foresaw the predicament of "the native" living in 1951 when He taught, through his Apostles, that there is no salvation for anyone outside the Roman Catholic Church, or without personal submission to the See of Peter. And yet, in some later conversation, the same people will reassure themselves that "the hairs of our head are numbered,"[39] and—"He marks the sparrow's fall."[40]

People generally were not taught, and so have no idea, of the rapid growth of the Church during the lives of the Apostles.

---

[39] Luke 21:18; Acts 27:34

[40] Matthew 10:29

They do not know that before the death of the last Apostle, Saint John, the Faith had been brought to every part of the known world. The world-wide spread of the Faith is called "the miracle of diffusion." When the modern Catholic thinks of the early Christians at all, he thinks of them as being only a few in number, and that few as the poor and illiterate. But that is not so. The Church had great successes, even in its the earliest days. In the centuries following the age of the Apostles, the Church continued to grow, despite the wholesale persecutions.

"The native in darkest Africa" figures so largely in the problem of salvation for the Catholic in our day because the average American looks upon Africa as a dark and primitive land, to which the Faith was never carried. Again, it is the contrary that is the truth. Saint Mark brought the Faith to Africa. He was the first Bishop of Alexandria. And Alexandria was a thriving city in his day, the seat of great culture. Men of intellect were attracted to it from all over the world because of its famous Catechetical School, which produced some of the greatest theologians of the Church. This was the school governed by Saint Clement of Alexandria and by Origen.

The spread of Christianity from Carthage, in northwest Africa (Alexandria is in northeast Africa), was so remarkable that Tertullian, who was a priest of Carthage, wrote, in 202 A.D., that throughout the cities of Africa, the Christians almost outnumbered the Pagans. Saint Cyprian, Bishop of Carthage, convened a synod there, sometime after 248, at which eighty-seven bishops were present.

The great Saint Augustine, renowned throughout all the Christian ages, was an African.

And so the "poor African native" *had* had the Faith, from its very source. So also had the native in Asia. And in Europe. And on all the adjacent islands. Cortes, way along in 1520, found the American Indian—in Central America—in possession of many religious truths, carefully preserved and handed down from generation to generation.

If there is one thing we at Saint Benedict Center have learned it is that the world is a very small place religiously, and that religious news travels, in one way or another, like lightning. Students who have come to us from all over the world have told us that the story of our fight for the pure orthodox doctrines of the Church reached even to the most remote parts of their countries.

We are but one human race, children of the same parents. It is evidence of loss of Faith and loss of true knowledge of God that men today question not only God's Power—to get His Truth to any and all lands—but His Goodness also—to leave men *of good will* without the means of salvation. Catholics in our time make themselves out to be more merciful, just and charitable than God. In their pride and weak Faith they forget that God, in His Omniscience, knows whether men would accept or reject the Church, were it offered to them, and that creatures are generally in the state they choose to be in. The fallen angels, for example, were they given a choice again, would once more choose Lucifer to the Eternal God. The souls in hell could not stand the pure white light of heaven for a single instant.

And so we return to consideration of the "plight of the poor native." The ancestors of "the native" had the Faith, we know. We have the word of many of the early Saints and Christian writers for that. Saint Justin Martyr, for instance, wrote, about 150 A.D.:

There is not any one race of men, barbarian or Greek, nay, of those live in wagons or who are nomads, or shepherds in tents, among whom prayers and Eucharists are not offered to the Father and Maker of the Universe, through the name of the crucified Jesus.[41]

Saint Clement of Alexandria, in Africa, writes, somewhat later:

The word of our Master did not remain in Judea, as philosophy remained in Greece, but has been poured out over the whole world, persuading Greeks and barbarians alike.[42]

The famous Origen, who at eighteen years of age became the head of the School of Alexandria, wrote, sometime after 203:

In all Greece and in all barbarous races within our world, there are tens of thousands who have left their national laws and customary gods for the law of Moses and the word of Jesus Christ.... And considering how, in so few years, in spite of the attacks made on us to the loss of life or property, and with no great store of teachers, the preaching of that word has found its way into every part of the world so that Greeks and barbarians, wise and unwise, adhere to the religion of Jesus, doubtless it is a work greater than any work of man.[43]

We know, then, that long ago the Faith was held and lost,

---

[41] *Dialogue with Trypho the Jew*, Chap. 117.

[42] *The Stromata, Book 1, Chap. 18.*

[43] *De Principiis*, Book 4, Chap. 1, n. 1-2

Gate of Heaven

in these lands where it had flourished so gloriously. Now, loss of Faith is always culpable. It is always man's fault, that is, when he has lost his God-given gift of Faith. This is the clear teaching of the Church. It is by man's sins—whether of neglect, sloth, indifference, worldliness, selfishness, vice—that he no longer believes.

And—and this is the significant fact with regard to the native—the sins of the fathers are visited upon their sons. "Like father, like son" is repeated for our reflection and chastisement in the stories of the human race in all generations. The sin of Adam and Eve is the "original sin" with which every child comes into the world, every man's inheritance from a sinful father. [44] The cities of Babylon and Jerusalem tell that tale. Chanaan was cursed for the sin of his father, Cham.[45] And on and on it goes. The men who followed Luther and Calvin, John Knox and Henry VIII, passed on to their children their sin. Their children are Protestants of our day, whose fathers lost the Faith for them.

We have actually been told by Liberal Catholics that we are wrong in calling the Protestants of our day *heretics*. "They are *not* heretics," we are told. "Their great-parents were, because they had the Faith and left it. But these descendants of theirs are innocent of heresy. They are living the religion their parents taught them, and in no sense should they be blamed for not having the Catholic Faith."

"But why should *you* be blamed and have to be baptized so as to be cleansed of a sin committed by Adam thousands of years ago?" we ask, in answer. "Were you not many times more innocent than the adult Protestant of our day? And yet if

---

[44] Romans 5:12-18

[45] Genesis 9:25

you had died unbaptized, with Adam's sin still upon your soul, you could not have entered heaven. The sins of the fathers are visited upon their children. It is up to the children to remove them. It is up to modern Protestants to come back to the true Faith. It is we who have charity, when we tell them that; you who lack charity, when you leave them in darkness."

This, Liberal Catholics refuse to see, mainly because they hold their Faith so lightly that they themselves have practically lost it.

It seems to me that if the modern Liberal Catholic would stop trying to pin the Infinite God down to his own sentimental standards of fair play, and humbly hearken to what He is saying, because it is God Who speaks, he might yet save his waning Faith in time to pass it down to *his* children—lest *they* become the "poor native" for succeeding generations.

Men who truly possess the Faith, and therefore knowledge of God as He really is, can be certain from this knowledge that God, when He sees good will and open hearts anywhere in the world, will find a way to get His Church there. He sent Saint Isaac Jogues and his companions—the eight North American Martyrs—to North America to bring Baptism and the Blessed Sacrament to the Indians. The only conspicuous fruit of their work was one little Indian girl, Kateri Tekakwitha.[46] God knew she would respond when the Faith was offered her, and give Him love in return for Love—as only those who hunger and thirst for God can.

God, Who is All Power and All Goodness, will bring visible means—His Priests—with visible signs—His

---

[46] Born at Ossernenon (Auriesville, NY) in 1656 and baptized at the age of 20, four years before her death. The "Lily of the Mohawks" was beatified June 22, 1980; her feast day is July 14.

Sacraments—to all who seek Him truly, in order that they may belong to His visible Church, and thus secure salvation. We know this, it is true, from our knowledge of God. We know it also because He has told us so, very clearly, in Holy Scripture.

It is told in the Acts of the Apostles (Chapter 10) that Saint Peter was sent to Caesarea for the sole purpose of baptizing Cornelius, a Gentile, and his family. Cornelius was a religious man, who feared God. He had taught all in his house to fear God. He gave alms to the people, and he was praying, always.

One day, God sent an angel to Cornelius, to tell him that God had heard his prayers, that his alms and his prayers had ascended to God, and that he must at once send men to Joppe to summon to his home Simon Peter. This Cornelius did, and when Saint Peter had made his journey from Joppe to Caesarea, he said to Cornelius:

Acts 10;29:...I came when I was sent for. I ask, therefore, for what cause you have sent for me?

30: And Cornelius said: Four days ago, unto this hour, I was praying in my house, at the ninth hour, and behold a man stood before me in white apparel, and said:

31: Cornelius, thy prayer is heard, and thy alms are had in remembrance in the sight of God.

32: Send therefore to Joppe, and call hither Simon, who is surnamed Peter: he lodgeth in the house of Simon a tanner, by the sea side.

33: Immediately therefore I sent to thee: and thou has done well in coming. Now, therefore, all we are present in thy sight, to hear all things whatsoever are commanded thee by the Lord.

34: And Peter opening his mouth, said: In very deed I perceive, that God is not a respecter of persons.

35: But in every nation, he that feareth him, and worketh justice, is acceptable to him.

Comment : The Catholic Liberal in our day—clerical or lay—would stop right here in the story of Saint Peter and Cornelius. The story is finished as far as the Liberal is concerned. He has, to his way of thinking, been assured of Cornelius' salvation. And nothing is farther from the truth. Cornelius has not yet been baptized. No man can, anymore, be saved without the Sacraments. We have but to read the words of Saint Peter in the verses which follow, in this same chapter of the Acts of the Apostles, to know this:

36: God sent the word to the children of Israel, preaching peace by Jesus Christ: (he is Lord of all).
37: You know the word which hath been published through all Judea: for it began from Galilee, after the baptism which John preached.

Saint Peter went on to instruct Cornelius and his family in the Faith of Jesus Christ. And "the Holy Ghost fell on all them that heard the word."

47: Then Peter answered: Can any man forbid water, that these should not be baptized, who have received the Holy Ghost, as well as we?
48: And he commanded them to be baptized in the name of the Lord Jesus Christ. Then they desired him to tarry with them some days.

The Liberal Catholics would have complimented Cornelius, and have left him unbaptized. Saint Peter complimented Cornelius, and opened to him the road to salvation, by the waters of Baptism. Peter, the first Pope, should know the explicit command of Jesus Christ. Thanks be to God, we know it, too, from him and from his successors in the Holy See. And also because the Holy Spirit has preserved it for us so beautifully in this chapter in the Acts of the Apostles.

Now, Cornelius did not live on a desert island, nor did he live in Africa. He could not perfectly be likened to "the poor native" who stirs up so much sympathy salvationally in the year of Our Lord, 1951. And so, almost as if for our benefit Holy Scripture gives us a native, in the desert, and an African!

We learn in the Acts of the Apostles (8;26) that God sent Philip way down to the south, from Jerusalem into Gaza, to find a lone Ethiopian, a eunuch, in order to baptize him. Philip was sent to the eunuch for no other reason than to baptize him.

Now, if it were enough for salvation to have baptism of desire, in the sense in which the Liberals of our day hold baptism of desire, certainly this eunuch had it. He was of good will, he sincerely desired God, and he was holy. However, all this was not enough—no more than it was enough for Cornelius, who also possessed these virtues. It still was necessary for the eunuch to be born again, of water and the Holy Ghost.

It was necessary for him to be baptized, and by *water*. *Baptism of desire is desire for Baptism of water.*

It is clear that God sent Philip on his long journey to the eunuch precisely in order to baptize him, because immediately after the baptism was administered, the Spirit of the Lord took Philip away.

Acts 8;26: Now an angel of the Lord spoke to Philip, saying: Arise, go towards the south, to the way that goeth down from Jerusalem into Gaza: *this is desert.*

27: And rising up, he went. And behold a man of Ethiopia, an eunuch, of great authority under Candace the queen of the

Ethiopians, who had charge over all her treasures, had come to Jerusalem to adore.

28: And he was returning, sitting in his chariot, and reading Isaias the prophet.

29: And the Spirit said to Philip: Go near, and join thyself to this chariot.

30: And Philip running thither, heard him reading the prophet Isaias. And he said: Thinkest thou that thou understandest what thou readest?

31: Who said: And how can I, unless some man shew me? And he desired Philip that he would come up and sit with him.

32: And the place of the scripture which he was reading was this: "He was led as a sheep to the slaughter; and like a lamb without voice before his shearer, so openeth he not his mouth.

33: "In humility his judgment was taken away. His generation who shall declare, for his life shall be taken from the earth?"

34: And the eunuch answering Philip, said: I beseech thee, of whom doth the prophet speak this? of himself, or of some other man?

35: Then Philip, opening his mouth, and beginning at this scripture, preached unto him Jesus.

36: And as they went on their way, they came to a certain water; and the eunuch said: See, here is water: what doth hinder me from being baptized?

37: And Philip said: If thou believest with all thy heart, thou mayest. And he answering, said: I believe that Jesus Christ is the Son of God.

38: And he commanded the chariot to stand still; and they went down into the water, both Philip and the eunuch: and he baptized him.

39: And when they were come up out of the water, the Spirit of the Lord took away Philip; and the eunuch saw him no more. And he went on his way rejoicing.

This is the story of the "native from darkest Africa" elaborately and clearly told at the very beginning of the Acts of the Apostles.

There is, we might reflect, the further lesson for us of the great singularity of this native in Holy Scripture. He was a eunuch, and therefore was not to be the father of any family or race. But so precious is the individuality of every man before God, so much does He love each of us for our own sakes, that He judges us not as a nation, or a group, or a family, but as persons. Each of us is given a "particular judgment" at the moment of our death. Each of us is personally responsible.

Every native of good will in the world some missionary will find, if the native is willing to take the Faith. The one native whom the Liberal Catholics have never been able to discover is the eunuch staring at them in this story in the Acts of the Apostles. When they say to us:

"What about the native in darkest Africa?"

(this is always a native they do not know really), our answer is, and must be:

"What about the native in Holy Scripture, and how do you explain him?"

Perhaps it were well to pause here for a moment to consider the question of "invincible ignorance."

A man who lives, let us say, in the United States, knows

that it is a governed nation. He knows that this government is for his good, and is indispensably so. He also knows that he must investigate, with reasonable diligence, its laws, because he must observe these laws, or else be punished for not doing so. There is no man who has not enough civic and social wisdom to get rid of his ignorance about the laws of his State.

Likewise, a man looking around the world knows that the world is governed by God. And with Christian challenges staring him in the face and shouting into his ears, he must know that this world is governed by Christ, true God and true Man. If he is to save his soul, he knows that he must investigate what are the laws of this government of Christ. And it is evident to him—or it should be—that the rules laid down for his salvation by Jesus Christ cannot be found in those Christian sects which speak without authority—and which disagree among themselves as to what the rules may be.

It could happen, with regard to a particular law, that the State might find that an individual was ignorant of it through no fault of his own. He would then be morally exonerated, but he would legally be punished, because that is the law.

For example, a man who did not know where he had to pay his income tax, and therefore avoided paying it, would not be excused for not having searched around until he had found out where to pay it. The officer of the law might sympathize with the man in his ignorance, but he would have to penalize him for not observing the law, or else it would be foolish for a State to make laws at all. If the State were to leave it to the sincerity of the citizens to imagine what civic laws should be— and then obey those they privately thought were for the public good—we would see the complete end of the common welfare, for which the State was instituted.

In absolute literalness, we must admit that it is possible for a human being to lose his soul without being guilty of any sin committed by himself. Christ laid down what the law of salvation was, and this law must be observed so as to secure salvation. Even the most Liberal Catholic theologians do and must hold that no unbaptized baby can see God in the Beatific Vision, because he has not fulfilled the law laid down for such beatitude. He has never been baptized.

The unbaptized baby is not in the least morally to blame, either for not observing the law, or for not knowing it. But if he is to be let in on the score of non-observance and ignorance, that is the end of the first law of salvation. To give weak efficiency to the State in making its laws is bad enough practice. To tell God, an omniscient Law-Giver, that He does not know how to make laws mercifully is complete and clear blasphemy.

If unbaptized babies can get into Heaven, Jesus Christ should have thought of this when He said: "Unless a man be born again of water and the Holy Ghost he shall not enter into the kingdom of heaven,"[47] and He should not have made this statement.

"In which case," Father Feeney said one day, "missionaries and priests and parents would not in the least bother to baptize babies since they would then know there were two ways of getting into heaven: one through the regenerative water of Baptism, and the other through the non-reception of Baptism, in the blissful state of not knowing it had to be received. This would be the end of law, and may I add, the end of Baptism. It would also be the end of all the other Sacraments for which Baptism is a prerequisite. In short order, it would be the end of Christianity.

"It is ten thousand times more merciful to let an

---

[47] John 3:5

unbaptized baby not see God forever than to blot Christianity off from the face of the earth. But that is what the pretended weepers over the invincible ignorant do, when they claim it to be an entrance qualification for the kingdom of heaven. It is our duty to take care of God's law, and let God's law take care of the baby.

"It is terribly surprising to find that a Catholic—who must admit that his unbaptized baby, who died, let us say, a childbirth, will never see God—holds that some unbaptized native who lived a few more years in the same condition, will. There is no doubt about it that solicitude for the salvation of the unbaptized native (which seems to be the only charitable solicitude which Liberal Catholics possess) is very soon in the United States of America going to lead over to allowing unbaptized babies to receive the Beatific Vision. Already, in Emmanuel College, a Catholic college taught by the Sisters of Notre Dame, and staffed theologically by some professors who are priests from Saint John's Seminary in Brighton, it is being hinted in religion classes that unbaptized babies may get into heaven through what is being called 'the illumination theory.' This can hardly be called Baptism of Desire, since the child does not even know its own desires. What it is is a new form of Baptism, a new substitute for the water prescribed by Christ. And very soon we may expect, in Catholic America, to find in our re-edited catechisms, four kinds of Baptism, instead of the present three: Baptism of water, Baptism of blood, Baptism of desire, and Baptism of illumination.

"This is the end of Baptism. The word is beginning now to have no meaning whatsoever. Let us pray that Our Holy Father will guard us from this blasphemous heresy, and preserve for us our one Lord, our one Faith, and our one Baptism."

God is an omniscient Law-Giver. He is omniscient both in knowing what laws are just, and in knowing how to phrase His laws, with perfect justice and charity. We must not tamper with these laws. If we do, we will not only lose natives on desert islands, we will lose whole nations to the Faith.

To repeat once again, if there is a native on a desert island, whom God knows is willing to receive the message of Christ, God will get him a missionary, just as He got Philip to the eunuch. If no missionary comes, it will be because God sees no missionary would be received, were he to come. The native will not be to blame morally, and will never be punished in hell for having rejected the Faith, because he did not, in fact, do so. It was only God Who knew he would. But he also will never receive the Beatific Vision because he neither had the Faith nor was baptized. And this is God's Justice.

During this past winter, students from Boston College have come to us with the news that some of the Jesuit Fathers were saying that Saint Benedict Center, in its stand on No Salvation Outside the Church, did not take into account the "salvific will" of God. The fact is that we *do* take into account the "salvific will" of God, but we take care to quote it the way it is expressed in Saint Paul.

The term "salvific will" is derived from a half-quotation of text in Holy Scripture:

1 Tim. 2;4: Who will have all men to be saved, and to come to the knowledge of the truth.

The Liberals quote the first half of this passage of Saint Paul, namely:

God wills all men to be saved,

and go on speaking about the "salvific will" of God. They neglect to finish the text:

and to come to the knowledge of the truth,

which can mean nothing else except:

and come to the knowledge of His Church,

which Saint Paul calls, in the very next chapter of Timothy (3;15):
...the Church of the living God, the pillar and ground of truth.

Now if, as the Jesuits say, God wills every man to be saved (whether or not he comes to the knowledge of the truth), how do they explain the beginning of Chapter 4, in this same Epistle of Timothy? It reads:

Now the Spirit manifestly saith, that in the last times some shall depart from the faith, giving heed to spirits of error, and doctrines of devils.[48]

It was precisely because the prince of devils, Lucifer, desired the prerogatives of God that he and his angels were damned for all eternity, and we have the devils, in hell. Modern Liberals actually hold that it is possible for a man holding "doctrines of devils" to be saved so long as he holds them "sincerely"!

---

[48] 1 Timothy 4:1

The "salvific will" of God could best be expressed this way:

God wills all men to come to the knowledge of the truth and thereby to be saved.

This is what Saint Paul's text means and says. Saint Thomas, in agreement with all the doctors, confirms this meaning in his Commentary on the First Epistle to Timothy. There is a sense in which it is wrong to say simply: "God wants all men to be saved," if you do not add, "and come to the knowledge of the truth." It is heresy to say that God wants all men, or any man, to be saved *without* coming to the knowledge of the truth.

Those who do not come to the knowledge of the truth, and do not enter the Church which was divinely instituted to preserve and teach it, cannot be saved. God has said so, and unless we are trying to establish a God to our own image and likeness, we had better stop tampering with the decrees that are Divine.

● ● ● ● ● ● ● ● ● ●

Perhaps, before closing this chapter, it might be well to add, by way of postscript, a word on the question which is second to "the native" in the minds of Catholics today.

"But Our Lord told us to judge not, that we be not judged," we are told. "And He told us to love our enemies."

It is true we should love *our* enemies. But *God's* enemies are a different matter. God's enemies are doing the work of the devil, and should we love the devil, or those he is bringing along to hell with him?

We do not have a right to judge a man's morals rashly; we never know what has been resisted, and what consented to. Only God knows the secrets of men's hearts, and we dare not pass false judgment on a man's drunkenness, anger, gluttony, pride, envy—or impute motives to him with regard to his sins.

But his belief in God, and his following of Jesus Christ are another matter. Our Lord Himself has told us:

John 3;18:...But he that doth not believe is already judged.

Our Lord has actually instructed us *how* to judge with regard to the things of God. When He said:

Matt. 12;30: He that is not with me, is against me,

He expected us to judge who were with Him, and who were against Him. When he admonished us to shake the dust from our feet against some, He presumed we should judge those to whom we should do this. When he commanded:

Matt. 7;6: Give not that which is holy to dogs; neither cast ye your pearls before swine, lest perhaps they trample them under their feet, and turning upon you, they tear you...

Jesus enjoined us to know those *who are dogs*, and those *who are swine*. We can know men who are dogs and men who are swine only by judging them to be such.

If a father has a little daughter whose innocence and sweetness and purity he wants to protect, how can he do so unless he judges those who would endanger it? Every one of us has had the experience, sooner or later, of being told by one of our parents, "Do not go with him—or her. They are not nice people. Have nothing to do with them." A parent who would not do this for a child, is not a good parent. And certainly this is judging.

And so if we have a pearl of great price to preserve—our Catholic Faith—which we should not cast before swine, how can we preserve it unless we judge who are swine?

"But I do not think you can win people by being so outspoken," we are usually told at this point. "I think you can convert many more by good example."

Howard Cannon once wrote an article in the magazine *From the Housetops*, showing that what modern Catholics are doing—under this silent-good-example policy—is to bring, not Jesus Christ, but *themselves* to those outside the Church. They are luring people into liking them, not into loving Jesus and Mary. Whether Catholics are good or bad, nice or not nice, pleasant mannered or unpleasant mannered, is no proof that the Catholic Church is the one true Church.

The Catholic Church is the one true Church because it was founded by Jesus Christ through His Apostles, with Peter and his successors as His Vicars and visible head, and with His promise that the gates of hell shall *never* prevail against it.

Chapter VI

The Church has not had a canonized saint among its popes since Pius V (1566-1572), almost four hundred years. There has not been a saint among the Popes from the sixteenth century until our own time. It seems very significant that Pope Pius X (1903-1914), who was beatified on June 3d, 1951[49], has been called the Pope of the Holy Eucharist and the great opponent of Modernism—which is our present-day Liberalism's ancestor. Little children can now go to Holy Communion as soon as they reach the use of reason; and every priest, before he is given Holy Orders, is obliged to take a solemn oath against Modernism.

Were Pope Pius X alive today, I am certain that there would not be one priest who would be allowed to be ordained until he had taken an oath against Liberalism, which is more endangering to the Church than even Modernism was in the days of that beautiful archbishop and father, Giuseppe Sarto, Pope Pius X.

Pope Pius X is also known as the "Pope of the Poor," an appropriate second title for the "Pope of the Blessed Sacrament." Poverty in material possessions can make one holy, if one wishes to be poor for Jesus' sake. But to be without spiritual food is destitution indeed. Certainly there are none so poor, none so bereft, none so abandoned, as those who have not the Bread of Life. Pope Pius X restored daily Communion once again to the Church, and so we who come after him have the privilege which the early Christians had, of receiving the Blessed Sacrament every day.

---

[49] Pope Saint Pius X was canonized on May 29, 1954.

I wish that we were also given the doctrines that go with the Holy Eucharist. The early Christians held all the dogmas clear and firm, and their reception of the Body and Blood of Jesus Christ, together with their devotion and realization of this Gift of God, raised up men and women who converted the world. They withstood the persecutions of three hundred years, and the blood of their martyrs became the seed of the Church. It never once occurred to them to think that the Bread of Life was meant for them alone. They knew it was meant for every man and woman, and their love was not satisfied until they had given their best gift to all mankind.

For almost two hundred years, Catholic theologians, with no claim in their lives to heroic sanctity, have been tampering with the dogmas of the Church, robbing them of their substance. They have been teaching a diluted Christianity, which has finally ended up in the outright heresy of our day—Liberalism. Every doctrine suffers from this heresy, and none so blasphemously as the doctrine of the Holy Eucharist and its necessity for the salvation of every human creature.

If only the Catholic people could again have strong, orthodox teachers, they would, in this Age of Mary, burn with the Faith, and spread it. Wars would cease, and peace would come. And this is the only way in which peace can possibly come to the world again.

We have but to listen to the way in which the early Christians prayed to realize how much we, in our time, have been cheated in doctrine. The first Christians were aware of many profound realities which our mediocre and weak religious instruction has kept hidden from us. When the early Christians said, "Give us this day our daily bread," this daily bread they understood to be the Holy Eucharist. We have been taught to think of it, in our day, as no more than the bread we eat at meals in our homes or in restaurants. Our Lord's hallowed petition has actually found its ways into economics courses in pagan colleges, and a well-known Catholic priest recently wrote, in a newspaper, two columns on its significance as the bread we earn by the sweat of our brow.

Saint Matthew records for us in his Gospel the words of Jesus teaching us how to pray, in that sublime praise and petition of God known throughout Christendom as "The Our Father."

Matt. 6;9: Thus therefore shall you pray: Our Father who art in heaven, hallowed be thy name.

10: Thy kingdom come. Thy will be done on earth as it is in heaven.

11: Give us this day our *supersubstantial bread*.

There is a footnote, in the Douay Version of the Holy Scripture, which explains:

Verse II: *Supersubstantial bread*. In Saint Luke, the same word is rendered *daily bread*. It is understood of the bread of life, which we receive in the Blessed Sacrament.

I know almost no Catholic who ever was taught that "give us this day our daily bread" had reference to the Holy Eucharist. And yet the Fathers and Doctors of the Church have written at length about it.[50]

---

[50] The *Fathers of the Church* are those teachers of the first six centuries, particularly, who were noted for the complete orthodoxy of their teaching, and some, for the extraordinary holiness of their lives. The *Doctors of the Church* were so declared because of the holiness of their lives and the great learning of their writings. There are, up to the present, 33 Doctors. The Church holds the Fathers and the Doctors up to us as our teachers.

Gate of Heaven

Saint Jerome—the great Doctor of the Church who translated the Holy Gospels from Greek into Latin—tells us that *give us this day our daily or supersubstantial bread* means that we ask, above all, for heavenly bread, the bread of the Eucharist.[51] Saint Ambrose[52], Saint Augustine[53], Saint John Chrysostom[54] have dwelt in their sermons and in their writings upon our daily bread, which is Jesus Christ, in the Blessed Sacrament. Catholics in our day, however, are not given these Doctors of the Church to read. In fact, comparatively few Catholics now know either that there are Fathers and Doctors of the Church or who these Fathers and Doctors are, much less that their orthodoxy has been confirmed by the Popes. We are given for instruction in our Faith merely the Baltimore Catechism—revised to suit modern Liberal interpretation—and a few present-day, popular, Liberal religious writers whose work will be discarded, along with their opinions, in a few years.

The Blessed Sacrament was the daily bread of the early Christians. Saint Luke tells us this in the Acts of the Apostles (2;46). And so does Saint Cyprian, a saint and martyr of the early Church:

> We ask that this bread may be daily given us, lest we, who are in Christ, and daily receive the food of the Eucharist, by the intervention of some grave fault, by abstaining and not communicating, should be kept back from the heavenly

---

[51] *Treatise of Saint Jerome, Book 3,#15*

[52] *Exposition of the Christian Faith, Chap. 9, #78*

[53] *Our Lord's Sermon on the Mount, Book 2, Chap. 7*

[54] *Homilies on Saint Matthew, Homily 49, #4*

Bread, and separated from the Body of Christ, when He Himself has admonished us saying, "I am the Bread of Life, Who came down from Heaven. If any man shall eat of My Bread he shall live forever."[55]

Ah, yes, we will be told by the Liberals, but Saint Cyprian wrote centuries ago. What have the *modern* theologians to say about it? The amazing progress of the last two hundred years, they will tell us, has changed the face of many things. We now really have the story. You cannot take the writings of the early Christians until you have read Harnack[56] (or some other morbid devotee of Higher Criticism).

What the Liberals are saying, in other words, is that we should not avail ourselves of the pure mountain water at its source, but should wait to drink from polluted waters, where the river has been sidetracked and is about to ooze out its existence in the stagnant stink of the swamp. Priests and laity alike have acquired this evaluation in secular colleges where professors—who see nothing uncivilized and depraved in atom bombing—loftily assure them that the early Christians lived, thought, and wrote in dark and comparatively unenlightened times.

This appraisal of early Christian life, even naturally speaking, is not a true one. The Greek culture, which was still prevailing at the time of Our Lord, was the highest natural culture the world has ever known. Christendom was trying to return to it, fourteen centuries later, through the Renaissance. This was unfortunate, for the Greek was an unbaptized and un-Eucharisted culture. And politically speaking, the Roman

---

[55] *Treatises 4,#18*

[56] Harnack, Karl Gustav Adolf von (1851-1930): Liberal Protestant heretic.

Gate of Heaven

Empire, in which the early Christians lived, was the most remarkably organized and most efficiently controlled system of government that ever has been achieved.

Vastly more important, however, than either of these considerations, is the fact that, from the standpoint of religion, it is blasphemously untrue to say that our age is more enlightened on the things of God than the age of the first Christians. The first Christians were enlightened by Our Lord Jesus Christ, Himself.

The Incarnation and Birth of Jesus Christ occurred in the "fullness of time." Religiously, everything since has been but a marking of time, so to speak. A marking of time, that is, until Christ once more returns, to judge the living and the dead. We are, or should be, hanging on for dear life to the period of time when Jesus Christ was with us—for if we miss its directions, its significance, we are done for. We fall back into a state worse than before.

So momentous was the impact of the Incarnation and Birth of Jesus Christ upon the world, that time was divided in terms of it. We speak of the time before Christ (B.C.), and of the time, not which is *after* Christ, but which is evermore *of* Christ. We live today in the nineteen-hundred-and-fifty-first year of Our Lord, 1951 A.D.

The time when God—Creator of heaven and earth and all things, Whose Thought maintains the planets and seas, mountains and lands, creatures and angels—surely that time, *when God became man and dwelt amongst us*, is the pivotal, central time toward which all before and everything after must ever point.

God the Father had been preparing the world for the coming of His Son from the tragic moment of Adam's and Eve's banishment from Paradise. The story of the Jewish people is the story of the getting ready for the coming of the Holy One. Three hundred years before the birth of Jesus, the Providence of God takes very definite shape in this work of preparation.

For instance, three hundred years before the Angel Gabriel's visit to Mary, and her conception of God's son through the Power of the Holy Ghost, seventy of the holiest and wisest Jewish doctors began the translation of the Old Testament from Hebrew into Greek. So wonderful was this translation when it was finished, so discernible is the work of the Holy Spirit in it, that it has been called inspired. The Old Testament itself is, of course, inspired in the first and direct meaning of the word, but so faultless and so pure was the choice of the Greek words for the Hebrew in this translation made in Alexandria in Egypt, that even *it* is thought to have been protectively inspired by the Holy Ghost. It is known to us as the "Septuagint," because of the seventy doctors who labored to complete it.

With the Septuagint, God's revelation was safe from the Jews, who would have distorted the Hebrew to fit their purposes when the Messiah they refused to acknowledge had come. The Jews eventually did distort the Old Testament, after the death of Our Lord, by the addition of the Talmud to the Pentateuch and by other ways, but the Sacred Books of the Old Law, by the Providence of God, had been made secure for the children of the Faith. They were preserved in Greek in the Septuagint and no harm could be inflicted on them by the Jews.

Even the conquest of Alexander, three hundred years

before the birth of Our Lord, and the subsequent Greekizing—Helenizing—of his vast territories, were used by God to prepare the world for his Son. Greek, as a language, lends itself to the most perfect communication.

Three hundred years, too, before the birth of Jesus in Bethlehem, the Jews, heretofore a despised people, suddenly found themselves liked, respected, welcomed. They traveled far and wide, in trade, unconscious (and sometimes conscious) missionaries, spreading the story of the Messiah to come, of the prophecies nearing fulfillment.

There was peace everywhere in the world, when Christ was born—the only time in history that this has been so. And all the prophecies perfectly were fulfilled, in the birth, life, and death of Jesus. It was, to repeat, the fullness of time.

The fullness of time! God walked His earth. He Who had brought them into being out of nothing, trod the land, looked at the sun, gazed at the stars, beheld the silver radiance of the moon. For the first time, God saw the beauty of His own creation, with the eyes of man.

And so filled with delight was Jesus with His own and His Father's handiwork, brooded over by the Holy Spirit, that He was always illustrating His utterances in terms of this marvelous creation:

Matt. 6;28: And for raiment why are you solicitous? Consider the lilies of the field, how they grow: they labour not, neither do they spin.

29: But I say to you, that not even Solomon in all his glory was arrayed as one of these.

30: And if the grass of the field, which is today...God doth so clothe: how much more you, O ye of little faith?

Religiously, there never will be a time again like to the time when God lived on earth. Those men who were alive then, or in the years immediately following, received the message of eternal life and what must be done to attain it, straight from the mouth of God. They are the ones we, almost two thousand years later, must listen to in order not to be fooled as to what is the truth and what is not the truth. If the world were many hundreds of years older than it is today, it would still have to return to the early Christians for the purity and orthodoxy of interpretation of what Jesus said and taught. The early Christians got it first-hand. They must ever be our most trusted teachers.

There is no such thing as an evolution of Christ's doctrine, or improvement upon it. To hold there is, is heresy. It is, actually, part of the heresy of Modernism, condemned by Pope Pius X. Christ's doctrine was perfect, as it came from Him, Who is God. It is perfect today, inasmuch as it remains untouched, exactly as He gave it, through His Apostles.

This precisely is the point for which Saint Benedict Center is fighting, and for which we are willing to go on fighting, no matter what the cost.

The pagan plague of "progress" has eaten into the Catholic Church in our day. Theologians no longer quote, as backing for their theories with regard to doctrine, the Saints and Fathers and Doctors of the Church. They quote other modern theologians, bitten like themselves with the poison of false interpretation and Liberal improvement upon doctrine. That it is possible to have deeper realizations of doctrine, I agree. But these realizations must be of old, unchanging truths, given to us for all time at the foundation of the Church, by Jesus Christ. They can in no way add to or take away from the original and real meaning of the dogmas.

Revelation—that is, the body of truth divinely proclaimed by Our Lord and Saviour Jesus Christ through His Apostles for our belief—was complete at the death of the last Apostle. We have no choice about believing or not believing the truths of Revelation. We must believe them, in order to be saved. Private revelations of the Saints are not imposed on us for belief. Pope Benedict XIV said with regard to them:

> Even though many of these revelations have been approved, we cannot and we ought not to give them the assent of divine faith, but only that of human faith, according to the dictates of prudence whenever these dictates enable us to decide that they are probable and worthy of pious credence.

The truths of Revelation, given to us by Our Lord, Jesus Christ, through His Apostles, are contained in what is called the "Deposit of Faith." The revealed truths in the Deposit of Faith have been gathered from two sources: the Sacred Scriptures and Apostolic Tradition. And these truths make up the Catholic Faith.

They were given by Our Lord to His Apostles to be zealously preserved and guarded by them and their successors, with the guarantee of infallibility, for the guidance of the Church, that all generations—in holding them—would possess the one true Faith and the key to salvation. They have been guarded, these sacred truths, with tenacity, and have been Divinely protected, else they would not have come down to us. We, in our turn, cannot relax our vigilance for an instant with regard to them. They should be guarded militantly. If there is no one else to do it—and it seems, as I write, that that is pretty close to being true—Saint Benedict Center, the Slaves of the

Immaculate Heart of Mary, will guard them—militantly. The Boston Heresy Case has provided all the evidence we, or anyone, need in order to know how abandoned pure Catholic dogma has become in our day.

"The doctrine of faith which God revealed," says the Vatican Council, "is proposed, not as a mere philosophical discovery to be elaborated by human minds but as the Divine Deposit delivered by Christ to his spouse, to be by her faithfully guarded and infallible declared."[57]

There has been no new revelation, may I repeat, since the death of the last Apostle, Saint John, who died in the year 99 A.D. The truths, the dogmas, which we must believe in order to be Catholics were all given to us by that time. The dogmas of the Church never can suffer change. They are today precisely what they were at the beginning of the Church. There are no new doctrines, and there can be no modifications of old ones.

Whenever a heretic challenged some revealed truth of the Faith, it became necessary for the Pope, either alone or together with his bishops in council, to re-express in more exact language the doctrine under attack, so that never again could there be any doubt about its meaning. This was done by definition.

We speak of the definition of a doctrine, or dogma. This does not mean that a new dogma is ever added to the Faith, or that something is added to an old dogma. It means merely that doubt or confusion has been cast on a doctrine, and it has become necessary for the Pope to remove the doubt and confusion. (When the Popes define there is no salvation outside the one true Church of Jesus Christ, it is sinful and heretical of modern theologians to make this infallible statement mean

---

[57] Vatican I *Session III, Chapter 3; Denzinger 1800*

anything less than what it states so clearly. By so doing, they throw new doubt and confusion upon an unmistakable and sacred doctrine.)

When it becomes necessary, then, for a Pope to define, he first gives the matter to his theologians for study. The theologians go back and examine the sources of the dogma in Holy Scripture and Tradition. They will find the doctrine stated there either explicitly or implicitly, and it is the truth either way. A dogma is *explicitly* expressed when it is brought out definitely in words, openly, plainly. A dogma is *implicitly* expressed when it is understood, but not specifically stated.

For instance, a dogma which is stated *explicitly* in Holy Scripture is:

And the Word was made flesh, and dwelt amongst us.

This doctrine is found in the beginning of the Holy Gospel according to Saint John (1:14). A doctrine which is not specifically stated in Holy Scripture, but which is understood, and therefore *implicitly* contained, is:

Jesus Christ had a human soul.

This truth was explicitly stated, or defined, by the Church in answer, as is generally the case, to heretical teaching—this time of Bishop Apollinaris, who had interpreted erroneously the passage from Saint John quoted above: "The Word was made flesh." Bishop Apollinaris maintained that Jesus had a human body (flesh), but no human soul, that His soul was supplied by the Spirit of the Word. The Church answered, through its second great General Council, at Constantinople, in the year 381, that if such were the case, Our Lord would not have been truly man. Since He *was* truly man, He had a human soul, like every other man. And so the Council proclaimed: "Jesus Christ is true God and true man."

I had an illustration one day of how close in time we Catholics are because of the unchanging oneness of the truths of the Faith. 381 A. D. and 1951 A. D. were as a moment. I found myself, one afternoon, "hearing" a little girl who is very dear to me recite her catechism lesson. I read from the small book she had put in my hand:

Q. Did Jesus Christ remain God when he became man?

A. Yes; He was always God.

Q. Was Jesus Christ always man?

A. No; only from the time of His Conception and Incarnation.

Q. What means the Incarnation?

A. That God the Son, the Second Person of the Blessed Trinity, *was made man.*

Q. What do you believe Jesus Christ to be?

A. True God and True Man.

There it was. All the way from the General Council of Constantinople it had come, this doctrine, implicitly contained in the Deposit of Faith. The words into which it had been cast in 381, simple, precise, unmistakable, were still guaranteeing and safeguarding the one, true Faith for a little girl, sixteen centuries later.

One of our boys, in a Sunday talk on Boston Common, likened the doctrines of the Church to a knitted robe. The dropping of one stitch means the eventual dropping of all. The very life of the Catholic Church depends on the successful defense of her doctrine.

Every dogma of the Catholic Faith is a revealed truth. One cannot choose one, discard another. Each is held on the Divine Word of God. To say that we approve some, and disapprove others, is to presume to stand in judgment on the veracity of God.

I wish it were possible, in this small book, to trace the stages of study in the definition of a doctrine. It is an enlightening experience. I once had this privilege, under a Jesuit priest, for a year. Nothing so reveals the integrity of the mind of the Church, and nothing so illustrates how perfectly one doctrine follows from another, how dependent one is upon the other, as such a study. I got from it a love of my Faith and an awareness of the oneness of Truth for which I have ever since been deeply grateful.

The Jesuit priest who opened up these riches of the Church for me failed to support Father Feeney and Saint Benedict Center in our fight against the Liberal Catholic assault on doctrine, when the opportunity was given him in the Boston Heresy Case. I have, ever since, never ceased to worry about his salvation. He taught his class that dogma can never change, and that it means precisely what it says. What I did not know was that he thought Catholic doctrine was for a few, and not for everyone, and that it does not mean what it says. His guilt is very great.

The most recently defined doctrine of the Church is the Assumption of Our Lady's body and soul into heaven. Everyone knows that antecedent to its definition, this doctrine was firmly believed. Its feast, on the 15 of August, was a Holy Day of Obligation. This feast is so old, and so universal in the Church, that some have said it is not only an apostolic doctrine but also an apostolic institution. We do know that it was celebrated by the Church after the Council of Ephesus, in 431.

Everyone knows, too, that Our Lady was intended, or at very minimum included, in the statement of the Sacred Scriptures: "...nor wilt thou give thy holy one to see corruption."[58]

Christians had long known that the Ark of the Covenant, which was made of imperishable wood, was a type of Our Blessed Lady, and she is so called in the Litany of Loreto:

Ark of the Covenant, pray for us.

Saint Thomas Aquinas, in his commentary on the Hail Mary, says:

The last curse common to man and woman, lies in this, that they must return to dust; and from this Mary was free. We believe that after her death she was restored to life and carried to Heaven, according to verse 8, Psalm 131, a text very often applied by early Christian writers to the two-fold resurrection of Our Lord and His Blessed Mother, she being the true Ark of the Covenant, which the Lord has sanctified.

Everyone knows, also, that Our Lady did not deserve to die—since she never was under the yoke of original sin—and having willed to die, in union with her Divine Son, it was no more fitting that she should see corruption than that He should. His Resurrection and Ascension are the complement of her Assumption into heaven, upon which glorious entrance of our Queen, there was "silence in heaven as it were for half an hour."[59] That is a long pause in eternity.

---

[58] Psalm 15:10 ; Acts 2:27 ; 13:35

[59] Apoc. 8:1

A *doctrine* or a *dogma* of the Church, then, *is a truth which has been revealed by God,* and must be believed by all Catholics. To deny a dogma whose belief is necessary for salvation is to be incapable of salvation, whether the denial is willful or not. A truth essential to salvation is not believed in, and that is the end of the matter.

A *definition of a dogma* is the more precise expression of the dogma. A definition is made by the Pope, or by an ecumenical or general council, acting with the Pope, and it is *infallible*. A definition is the last word on the subject. It never can make a doctrine more obscure, since its very purpose is to clarify. Each word in a definition is significant. There is always an economy of words in a definition, because truth is simple. We have an example of this in the doctrine: Extra Ecclesiam Nulla Salus: Outside the (Catholic) Church there is No Salvation.

An *Ecumenical or General Council* is a council summoned by the Pope, or by a ruler in the name of the Pope. It is made up of Bishops of the whole world—and other high ranking prelates with a right to vote, such as abbots, etc. Its decrees are not binding until approved by the Pope. The council is subject to the Pope, but the Pope is not subject to it. Its decrees, when they are confirmed by the Holy See, *are infallible*. There have been no more than twenty such councils in the history of the Church[60], from 325, when the first one occurred, to 1870, when the last one adjourned, its work incomplete.

The origin of councils is derived from the Council of the

---

[60] The Second Vatican Council (1962-65), was the 21st council of the Church.

Apostles, in the year 52, when all the Apostles came together, at Jerusalem, under Saint Peter, to talk over the affairs of the Church. The story of this first council of the Church is told in the Acts of the Apostles, Chapter 15.

The councils are an Apostolic institution, and the Apostles, when they instituted them, acted under the commission they received from Christ; otherwise they could not, as Bishop Hefele[61] says, have published the decisions of their council with the words, "It seemed good to the Holy Ghost and to us." They must have been convinced that the Lord of the Church had promised and had granted His Spirit to the assemblies of the Church.

Later councils have acted and spoken in the same conviction, that the Holy Ghost governed the Church's assemblies. This was the teaching of all the ancient Fathers of the Church. Pope Saint Gregory the Great even compared the authority of the first four general (or ecumenical) councils with the importance of the four holy Gospels.

The Church began on Pentecost. Pentecost is the birthday of the Church of Jesus Christ, and on it was fulfilled the promise of Jesus that He would send the Spirit of Truth Who would teach the Apostles and Disciples all truth.

Ten days after Our Lord ascended into heaven, when the Jews were beginning the celebration of the Jewish feast of Pentecost—on the same day that the Old Law had been given to Moses on Mount Sinai—the Holy Ghost came down upon the Apostles and Our Lady, in the Cenacle, while they were persevering in prayer. The Holy Spirit came in the form of tongues of fire, with the sound as of a rushing of a mighty wind. The Apostles went forth, from that hour, to preach the Gospel to men of every nation, whom they found gathered in

---

[61] Hefele, Karl Joseph von (1809-93): Bishop of Rottenburg, Historian.

Jerusalem from all parts of the Roman Empire for the feast of Pentecost. Three thousand were converted by Saint Peter that first day, and were baptized in the Name of the Father, and of the Son, and of the Holy Ghost.[62]

In the Acts of the Apostles, in Holy Scripture, Saint Luke relates the history of the Church in the years which followed upon this first Christian Pentecost. Over and over again, Saint Luke speaks of the sacred trust which was the Apostles' of preserving the *integrity* of the sacred Deposit of Faith, and of guarding these Divinely revealed truths against a shadow of change. The vigilance of the Apostles for the pure teaching of the doctrines of the Faith was as great as their care that the Church be sinless. They were obliged to enact severe penalties for anyone who would either reject or corrupt any part of the Deposit of Faith. They termed such rejection or corruption "blasphemy." We have often conjectured at Saint Benedict Center on what the Apostles would say and do to the theologians of our day who so blasphemously distort the sacred and solemn doctrine: Outside the Catholic Church there is No Salvation.

Since the death of the Apostles, only the Pope has personal infallibility in the Church. While the Apostles lived, each Apostle had personal infallibility. No one but Peter, however, had primacy of jurisdiction—over the whole Church, and over them.

When the Pope defines, in union with a council of his bishops, the principle of infallibility is the whole gathering of bishops, with the Pope as their head. Apart from the bishops, the Pope can be the principle of infallibility, all by himself, as I explained in an earlier chapter. No bishop has this prerogative. The Pope, therefore, is infallible in two ways: when he is acting

---

[62] Acts 2:41

corporately as the head of all his bishops in assembly, or when he is acting singly, by himself, as head of the Church—provided he makes it clear that he is speaking *ex cathedra*.

The Apostles were the true teachers of the pure doctrine of Jesus Christ. Their teachings were regarded as holy and *unchangeable*. They insisted *on unity of Faith* among the Christians, and on a full acceptance of *every single dogma of Faith*. Anyone who refused to take all the doctrines was immediately excommunicated, was called a heretic, and was shunned by the faithful. Saint John would not stay under the same roof with the heretic, Cerinthus. Saint John entered the public baths one day, and in some chance conversation he learned that Cerinthus was in the building. He left at once, denouncing the heretic, and saying that he could not bear that one roof should cover them both.[63] This was the same Saint John whose message to the world was: "Little children, love one another."[64] By the joining of this incident and this exhortation, we begin to see what Christian love really means.

The Apostles foretold that heresies would come in the Church:

1 Cor. 11;19: For there must be also heresies: that they also, who are approved may be made manifest among you.

Saint Paul meant, by this last, that heresies, instead of harming, would be of benefit to the Church, serving as a test of orthodoxy. As Saint John said, the heresies would show who were, and who were not—and who had never really been—of the Fold of Christ:

---

[63] Saint Eusebius, *Ecclesiastical History*, III, XXVIII, 1-6 ; IV, XIV, 6 ; VII, XXV, 2-3

[64] I John 4:7

Gate of Heaven

1 John 2;19: They went out from us but they were not of us. For if they had been of us, they would no doubt have remained with us: but that they may be manifest, that they are not all of us.

Faith comes from hearing. Mr. Arnold Lunn—who wrote a book on how he, by reading, rationalizing, and remembering, came into the Church—might have a little difficulty admitting this, but nevertheless it is the way the Church began. Our Lord said to his Apostles: "Go forth and *teach* all nations,"[65] and that is precisely what they did. That first Pentecost, and all the days thereafter, the Apostles preached the three great central truths of the Faith: the Incarnation—that is, the Conception and Birth of Jesus—His Passion and Death; and His Resurrection and Ascension. The Apostles gave instructions on Baptism, on Penance, on the Holy Eucharist, and on justification by Faith and works.

There is, I would like to stress, a distinction between *justification* and *salvation*. Justification, strictly speaking, is so far away from salvation that when Our Lord descended into "the Limbo of the Just"[66] at the moment of His death, this is referred to in the Apostles' Creed as:

"He descended into Hell."

Justification is a requirement for salvation, but it is not salvation itself. Justification, while one is in this life, can be lost. Salvation, which is of the life to come, can never be lost, once one has achieved it. Man can be justified in this life. He is

---

[65] Matthew 28:19

[66] Ephesians 4:9-10

saved only in the next, and only when he passes from this life to the next in a state of justification.

Justification puts us in the state of sanctifying grace, that is, in a state of Divine relationship towards God wherewith we deal with Him in terms of a Justice to which we were hitherto in no wise entitled.

In the beginning of our doctrinal defense, we were amazed beyond belief in the controversy with Father Philip J. Donnelly, S. J., to discover that Father Donnelly had confused justification and salvation. This controversy with Father Donnelly grew out of his reply to Raymond Karam's article quoting the Fathers and Doctors of the Church on salvation, which appeared in our magazine, *From the Housetops*.[67]

But to go on, the Apostles, after Pentecost, gave instructions also on the doctrines relative to the forgiveness of sins, our resurrection from the dead at the end of the world, and our final judgment. All these doctrines and instructions were contained in the articles of belief embodied in what we know as "The Apostles' Creed."

The *Gospels* and the *Epistles* were written by the Apostles so as to give permanence to their oral instructions. Oral teaching easily can be forgotten or distorted in the re-telling. Too, the Apostles wished to have a constant reminder of their instructions in the hands of the people. We are told by Eusebius, an early historian of the Church, concerning the writing of Saint Matthew's Gospel:

Matthew, who had originally taught among the Hebrews, when he was on the point of departure to carry the truths of the Gospel also to others, composed his Gospel in the

---

[67] The article "Liberal Theology and Salvation" appeared in the December 1948 issue of "From the Housetops."

vernacular tongue of those from whom he was about to part, that thus might be supplied the want of further instruction during his absence.

Saint Paul, because of the excellence, thoroughness, and clarity of his teaching, is frequently called the first theologian of the Church. He had had careful academic training as a Jew. Saint Paul was born in Tarsus, in Cilicia, and when he had completed a classical education there, he was sent by his family to Jerusalem, to study under Gamaliel, the master. Saint Paul was a Pharisee, and it was the Pharisees who believed that the Jews should not mix with those of other religions, if they wished to preserve the pure orthodoxy of their faith. (They were against interfaith Movements!) The Pharisees were the opposite of the Sadducees, who were the free-thinkers among the Jews.

Saint Paul, by his intellectual gifts and great talents, his intense energy and strength, his deep love of Our Lord and intimate union with Him, was better fitted than any of the Apostles for the mission of *theologian*. It is generally admitted that Saint Paul's method of expounding Christian doctrine is superior to that of the other Apostles in clearness of arrangement and thoroughness of handling. The Doctors of the Church are constantly going back to him, constantly using him for reference. No one has been able to exhaust him. Saint Thomas Aquinas built his *Summa Theologica* on the teachings of Saint Paul. He is referred to by holy writers simply as "The Apostle."

Now, this same Saint Paul's ever-recurring message was a plea, a warning, a demand for the preservation of the sanctity of doctrine. Do not tamper with doctrine! he beseeched. Let not the Word of God be changed to suit the tastes of men. In season and out of season he implored and pounded this necessity into the minds of his people. And he himself wrote in such a way that the Divine doctrine of Jesus Christ had all the protection of concise, comprehensive, and dogmatic composition.

The writings of the *Apostolic Fathers*—those Fathers who were the immediate disciples of the Apostles—show that they made every effort to preserve the method of teaching of the Apostles.

In the fifth century there lived a monk and simple priest named Vincent of Lerins. He wrote a book for the security of his own faith, so he says, by recalling and having at hand what the Apostles and Fathers had written as to how *private individuals and the simple faithful* should behave in the presence of prevalent heresies. This book is called the *Commonitory* of Saint Vincent Lerins. In it Saint Vincent brings out the point which I have been trying to stress in this chapter—that is, that when there is a question of what is true doctrine, a Catholic has only to go to antiquity in the Church—not to modernity—to know what is orthodox. He has only to return to those men who sat at the feet of Jesus and who taught in what is known—by reason of God's visible presence among them—as the fullness of time.

Saint Vincent Lerins' book, since it is an exposition of doctrine, is filled with the teaching of Saint Paul. Saint Vincent beautifully portrays for us Saint Paul's vigilance for the preservation of the truths in the Deposit of Faith, and gives us an example of his own teaching, in the following passages:

> *"O Timothy, keep that which is committed to thy trust, avoiding the profane novelties of words..."* (1 Tim. vi, 20). Who at this day is Timothy, but either generally the

universal Church, or especially the whole body of prelates, who ought either themselves to have a sound knowledge of Divine religion, or who ought to infuse it into others?...*Depositum custodi.* What is the *depositum*? It is that which has been entrusted to thee, not what has been found out by thee: what thou hast received, not what thou hast thought out; a matter not of ingenuity, but of learning; not of private adoption, but of public tradition; a thing brought to thee, not brought out by thee: wherein thou must be not an author, but a keeper, not an originator, but a pursuer: not leading, but following. *Keep*, he says, *the deposit: preserve the talent of the Catholic faith, inviolate and pure.* Let what has been entrusted to thee remain with thee, be delivered by thee. Thou has received gold, give back gold. I will not that thou offer me one thing for another, and have the face, instead of gold, to present me with lead, or cheat me with brass. I want not the appearance of gold, but its reality.

Keep that which is committed to thy trust, avoiding the profane novelties of words! Preserve the Catholic Faith, inviolate and pure!

How far away from this sacred commission the custodians of the Faith have gone in our day has been made woefully manifest in the story of the Boston Heresy Case. The Catholics of Saint Benedict Center literally have been made to stand alone and be persecuted for dogma. As far as we ourselves are concerned, we rejoice that to people so personally unworthy such a sacred privilege should come. We are grateful to the dear Mother of God for such trust, and we pray that some day she may give us the further favor of shedding our blood for the truths of Jesus Christ.

But, as far as the Church is concerned, we feel that never before has the Bride of Christ fallen upon such evil days. Never before have wicked men dared to utter such profane novelties of words, to be not keepers, but originators of dogma, not followers of the Word, but leaders; offerers of the brass of heresy, in place of the gold of pure Catholic truth.

Never before have theologians so betrayed the Faith, and this at a time when the world can be saved from destroying itself in no other way than by the one true Church of Jesus Christ. These evil theologians not only are not bringing the Catholic Church to the poor people outside it, they are actually taking it away from those inside it. They are making meaningless the dogmas which protect it. They are steadily sapping its life, stealing its vitality, robbing its truth.

We have received at Saint Benedict Center during this past month, four Catholic magazines and one Catholic newspaper which contain articles purporting to explain the two clear, simple doctrines: there is no salvation outside the Catholic Church nor without personal submission to our Holy Father, the Pope. One magazine was French, sent us from Paris. This turned out to be worse by far than its American counterparts. The maze of empty phrases, false distinctions, heretical statements in each of the five writings was clearly diabolical. That was all that *was* clear in the articles. We had no notion, when we finished, what the writers were saying other than that they were endeavoring to prove that the dogma: "There *is* No Salvation Outside the Catholic Church" really means: "There is salvation outside the Catholic Church."

With regard to the authors, themselves, however, it was very clear that each of the priests writing—French as well as American—had lost his Faith; or else was thoroughly dishonest. In either case, he is well on his way to losing his soul

140   *Gate of Heaven*

if he does not, before he dies, stop his diabolical reasoning and profess the pure Faith of Jesus Christ.

The United States has never had a native-born canonized saint.[68] But France is the land of saints. France was known in the days of Faith as the "eldest daughter of the Church." I know she has been a wayward daughter for a long time, but Our Lady came to Bernadette there in the last century[69], and the Little Flower of Jesus[70] lived and died in France during the lifetime of many who may read these words. We never dreamed that the Church in France would allow an article on salvation so heretical as the one which was sent us, written by a French Dominican, to pass ecclesiastical censorship. A young seminarian forwarded it to Dr. Maluf, at the Center.

This article from France—had we not the promise of Christ that the gates of hell will never prevail against the Church—would spell the end of the Faith. It leaves no need whatsoever for the Catholic Church. It promises salvation without that Church to everyone: Hindu, Mohammedan, Buddhist, Protestant, Jew—just as they are.[71]

For the past one hundred and fifty years, at least, what has been taught in American seminaries, and in most Catholic

---

[68] Saint Francis Xavier Cabrini (1850-1917) was the first American citizen canonized in 1946. She was though, born in Italy. Since 1951 (the first printing of this book) there has been one "native-born canonized saint," Saint Elizabeth Ann Seton (1774-1821), canonized Sept. 14, 1975.

[69] Apparition at Lourdes, France (Feb. 11 to July 16, 1858). Saint Bernadette Soubirous (1844-79): canonized 1933.

[70] Saint Therese of Lisieux (1873-97): canonized May 17, 1925.

[71] The late, French Archbishop Marcel Lefebvre, writing in his book: *A BISHOP SPEAKS-Writings and Addresses 1963-75*, has this to say on the subject, p.153, "One may be saved within Protestantism, within Buddhism, within any religion soever, but one cannot be saved by that religion!"

seminaries of the world, is that when you say "Outside the Church there is No Salvation," you must not take those solemn words as the ancient Church, close to Christ and His Apostles, took them—and as the Church universally taught them over eighteen centuries. You must now distinguish what you mean by "the Church."

There is, say these theorizers of the last one hundred and fifty years, both the *soul* of the Church and the *body* of the Church, and some not belonging to the body might be said to belong to the soul. This expression: *soul of the Church*, first used among professional theologians, crept out and was finally given to the common people as a doctrinal phrase. Indeed, it went even further,—until it was the only membership in the Church preached as *necessary*.

The expression "the soul of the Church" is but a metaphor. It was never intended to be used in more than a metaphorical sense, and that was the sense in which Saint Augustine first used it. We could say that a martyr who had the choice between waiting for Baptism, or being martyred for professing he was going to receive it, could, by the shedding of his blood, be said to belong in some way to the Church, and the phrase "the soul of the Church" could in that instance be used. It was never intended to be a partitioning of the Church into two parts, soul and body, of which the fuller members belong to both parts, and the lesser members to just one of the parts. But that is the way it is being used by the Liberal teachers of theology in the seminaries of the United States, so as to save embarrassment from having to teach Protestants unequivocally where it is they must be saved.

Orthodox doctrine can never change. Unsound theological opinion can change. And so we find the latest Liberals now discarding the distinction and evasion: "The soul of the Church." Typical of the Liberal theologians who have done this is Father Joseph Clifford Fenton, Editor of the *American Ecclesiastical Review,* who, with Father Francis Connell, C.SS.R., is supposed to be one of the conservative theologians at Catholic University.

It is well known that Pope Pius XII, in his encyclical on the *Mystical Body*[72], insists that the only true sense in which we can use the phrase, "soul of the Church," is to apply it to the Holy Spirit. It is the Holy Spirit Who *is* the Soul of the Church. There is no "soul of the Church" in the sense in which it was formerly (erroneously) understood. This leaves the heretics and infidels out, since in no way can they be said to belong to the *body* of the Church.

And so we have Father Fenton now writing in the *American Ecclesiastical Review* that the phrase, "soul of the church," should be used no longer. Father Matthew Smith, of the Denver Register, another supposed orthodox theologian, agrees with him. But all three priests, Father Fenton, Father Connell, and Father Smith, are still determined to allow some people not in the Church to get into heaven. In the pre-war days of our generation, they used to say—may I repeat:

With regard to the doctrine "Outside the Church there is No Salvation," that depends on what you mean by *the Church*.

The new version is:

With regard to the doctrine "Outside the Church there is No Salvation," that depends on what you mean by outside. All have to belong to the body of the Church to be saved.

---

[72] *Mystici Corporis,* June 29, 1943

And so, to get around that, Father Fenton now makes the distinction between:

> *Explicitly* belonging to the Church,
> and
> *Implicitly* belonging to the Church.

And this sinful and fraudulent distinction allows the same people who got out of being Catholics, by way of being part of the soul of the Church, now to get out of the challenge by being "implicitly" in the Church. Some Liberal priests have even gone so far as to say that this applies to some who would violently refuse the Church were it offered to them! These latter still belong to it, whether they know it or not, because they have some vague desire to go to heaven when they die and to lead (their own idea of) a moral life here on earth.

These are *implicit* members of the body of the Church, the Liberal theologians now tell us. The rest of us are *explicit* members.

The phraseology has changed. The heresy remains unaltered.

Chapter VII

Twelve years ago, in 1939, Father Leonard Feeney wrote, in his book, *You'd Better Come Quietly,* the following words:

Our minds, weary of climbing without pictures to assist us, through the tenuous droves of spirits that lie above us in the nine worlds of angel, are refreshed once more with an imaginative picture of something we know, love and have seen, before we step across the threshold of creation into the Ecstatic Essence of God. We find a girl again; with hands and eyes and hair, and a heart; airing her maiden-mother manners at the summit of all creation, constituted Queen of the Universe, with dominion over all angels and all men, more beautiful in her single reality, more pleasing to God, more full of Grace, than all the rest of creation put together. She is "beautiful as the moon, chosen as the sun, mighty as an army set in array." She is the Queen of Angels. She is the Mother and the Queen of Men. She originated on this little planet of ours, pertains to our race, our kind, is related to us not by the angelic ties of love and thought, but by the very fibres of flesh and blood.

Her alliance to God is threefold. She is the Daughter of the Father, the Spouse of the Holy Spirit, and the Mother of the Son. She presents all creation with a baby, whose name in Eternity is God, and whose name in time is Jesus.

She is the Mother of Divine Grace, powerful in her intercession. She is not God, she is the *Gate to God*, the Gate of Heaven. There is no passing to Eternal Life except through her. She is understanding, innocent, marvelously simple and unsuspicious, tender towards sinners. She takes us each by the hand and leads us to the Beatific Vision, and shares the radiant beauty of Christ's human nature begotten in her womb.

One cannot escape her. One cannot get into Heaven except through the Gate!

"You'd better come through the Gate!" God says to each of us. "Hesitations, incertitudes, nervousness, suspicions, doubts, what good do these do either a man or an angel?"

"You'd better come through the Gate...!

"And...*You'd Better Come Quietly!*"[75]

So wrote Father Feeney, years ago. And so wrote and preached the Fathers and the Doctors of the Church, long before Father Feeney. Saint Louis Marie Grignon de Montfort, who was canonized[76] by our present Holy Father, Pope Pius XII, wrote in his book, *True Devotion to the Blessed Virgin*:

It is an infallible mark of eternal condemnation to have no esteem and love for the holy Virgin; while on the other hand, it is an infallible mark of predestination[77] to be entirely and truly devoted to her.[78]

The figures and words of the Old and New Testaments prove this. The sentiments and the examples of the saints confirm it. Reason and experience teach and demonstrate it. Even the devil and his crew, constrained by the force of

---

[75] The Leonard Feeney Omnibus, *Sheed and Ward, 1944, Page 165*

[76] Saint Louis Marie Grignon de Montfort (1673-1716): canonized 1947.

[77] This is another infallible Dogma of the Church that has been attacked, undermined, and disbelieved by many in the Church today.

[78] *True Devotion to Mary*, #30

truth, have often been obliged to avow it in spite of themselves. Among all the passages of the holy Fathers and Doctors, of which I have made an ample collection in order to prove this truth, I shall for brevity's sake quote but one: "To be devout to you, O Holy Virgin," says Saint John Damascene, "is an arm of salvation which God gives to those whom He wishes to save."

Mary is the Gate of Heaven. The elect[79] are the children of Mary. So believed Saint Augustine, Saint Cyril of Jerusalem, Saint Ephrem, Saint Germanus, Saint John Damascene, Saint Anselm, Saint Bernard, Saint Bernardine of Sienna, Saint Thomas Aquinas, Saint Bonaventure. Saint Alphonsus de Liguori has written, in his book *The Glories of Mary,* a chapter on "Mary, Our Salvation," in which he gives the testimony of the saints, "in order to show how unanimous the various writers have been one the subject." He quotes Saint Anselm: "that as it is impossible for one who is not devout to Mary, and consequently not protected by her, to be saved, so is it impossible for one who recommends himself to her, and consequently is beloved by her, to be lost."

Saint Antoninus, says Saint Alphonsus, repeats the same thing and almost in the same words: "As it is impossible for those from whom Mary turns her eyes of mercy to be saved, so also are those towards whom she turns these eyes, and for whom she prays, necessarily saved and glorified." Saint Bonaventure writes:

He who neglects the service of the Blessed Virgin will die in his sins...He who does not invoke thee, O Lady, will

---

[79] The teaching that, God, by the eternal resolve of His will, predetermined certain men to eternal blessedness.

never get to heaven...Not only will those from whom Mary turns her face not be saved, but there will be no hope of their salvation.

Saint Alphonsus quotes Saint Hilary: "However great a sinner he may have been, if a person shows himself devout to Mary, he will never perish." Saint Alphonsus then goes on to say:

For this reason the devil does his utmost with sinners in order that, after they have lost the grace of God, they may also lose devotion to Mary. When Sara saw Isaac in company with Ismael, who was teaching him evil habits, she desired that Abraham would drive away both Ismael and his mother Agar: *Cast out this bond-woman and her son.* She was not satisfied with the son being turned out of the house, but insisted on the mother going also, thinking that otherwise the son, coming to see his mother, would continue to frequent the house. The devil, also, is not satisfied with a soul turning out Jesus Christ, unless it also turns out his Mother: *Cast out this bond-woman and her son.* Otherwise he fears that the Mother will again, by her intercession, bring back the Son. "And his fears are well grounded," says the learned Paciucchelli: for he who is faithful in serving the Mother of God will soon receive God Himself by the means of Mary."

This, may I say, explains as nothing else the tragedy of the absence of real devotion to Mary, God's Mother, in Protestant communities. Mary does not dwell in Protestant Churches. No Protestant would claim that she does. Mary is ever to be found with her Son, and Jesus is not present on the altars of the

Protestant Churches. He is not tabernacled there, in the Holy Eucharist. The Reformation rejected the Holy Sacrifice of the Mass and the Eucharistic Presence of the Body, Blood, Soul and Divinity of Our Lord Jesus Christ for purposes of Sacrifice, Sacrament and Communion.

The Protestant people are perpetually disturbed by what they term the Catholics' "excessive devotion to Mary." Whole chapters and sections of Protestant writings are given over to discussion of Catholic devotion to Mary—under the heading "Mariolatry," worship of Mary. All of the Protestant feeling of centuries, all of the Protestant errors with regard to Mary, broke out afresh a year ago, when Pope Pius XII defined the doctrine of Our Lady's Assumption into heaven. In Boston, a Protestant minister bought a large space in the daily newspapers in order to decry the Pope's definition of the Assumption; and in order to tell the Boston people that Our Lady was not a virgin, that Jesus was but one of many children, and that Mary was the mother of Christ but not the mother of God; that she was not immaculately conceived, and neither was she assumed into heaven. The only serious challenge this blasphemous utterance received was from the little Catholic group at Saint Benedict Center.

Perhaps I had better pause, in my portrayal of Our Lady as the Gate of Heaven, to speak of her as the Mother of Jesus, the Mother of God.

In the *Saint Andrew Daily Missal,* under the date of September 8th and the caption, "The Nativity of the Blessed Virgin Mary," there is the following notation:

Mary is inseparable from Jesus in the divine plan, wherefore the Liturgy applies to her what Holy Scripture says of the eternal Wisdom which is the Word "by whom all was made." Like Christ, the Virgin presides over the whole work of creation, for having been chosen from all eternity to give us the Saviour, it is she, with her Son, whom God had chiefly in view when He created the world.

It is she, with her Son, whom God had chiefly in view when He created the world! Mary, of Nazareth!

She is foretold in the beginning of the Holy Scriptures, in the Book of Genesis. She it is who will crush the head of Satan, and do battle for the souls of men.

Gen. 3;15: I will put enmities between thee and the woman, and thy seed and her seed: she shall crush thy head, and thou shalt lie in wait for her heel.

She is the prophecy of the Prophets.[80] She is the song of David.[81] David danced in the street before the Ark of the Covenant[82], when foreknowledge was given him that from Mary, the grace-filled daughter of his house, would come the Saviour of the world.[83]

She is the weeping of Sara, and Rebecca, and Rachel; of Jephte's daughter, and all the daughters of Israel. She is the answer to their cry. In her are their hopes fulfilled; in her their longing allayed. From her, the Redeemer of men was born.

"Hail, full of grace," the Angel Gabriel greeted her. "The

---

[80] Isaias 7:1-17; Micheas 5:2-3; Jeremias 31:22

[81] Psalms 44:18 ; 65:16

[82] II Kings 6:14

[83] Luke 1

Lord is with thee: blessed art thou among women."

"Blessed art thou among women," cried her cousin Elizabeth, whose own child, as yet unborn, was filled with the Holy Ghost at the approach and salutation of Mary. "Blessed are thou among women and blessed is the fruit of thy womb. And whence is this to me that the mother of my Lord should come to me?"

"Holy Mary, Mother of God," prayed the Church at the Council of Ephesus, "pray for us sinners, now and at the hour of our death. Amen."

From the salutation of Gabriel, the cry of Elizabeth, the petition of Ephesus, there was made the prayer which has ever been upon the lips of Catholic people, in the tender outpourings of their hearts to their Mother, in the time of their every need—the *Hail Mary*.

God will be worshipped, and the Mother of His Son venerated, whether men will it or men rue it. In the days preceding the preaching of Jesus, His precursor, Saint John the Baptist, cried out to his people:

Luke 3;8: Bring forth therefore fruits worthy of penance; and do not begin to say, We have Abraham for our father. For I say unto you, that *God is able of these stones to raise up children to Abraham.*

Just as God is able of stones to raise up children to Abraham, so is He able to wring from the earth, no matter now hard the hearts of men, adoration and praise worthy of Him in the Godhead, and praise and petition worthy of Mary in her divine motherhood. Perfect love and adoration are given to Him in the Holy Sacrifice of the Mass, and perfect praise and reverence are given to her in the *Hail Mary*.

It is as impossible to count the *Hail Marys* which have passed from the lips of men to the throne of the Queen of Heaven, as it is to number the grains of sand on the seashore. They are countless and ceaseless, these prayers which rise to Mary, not from the worldly powerful—who are as passing clouds, but from the spiritually powerful; from the least who shall be first, from the meek who shall possess the land, from the clean of heart who shall see God.

Mary's labor was not in the bearing of her Divine Son. He came through her body as light through a window. Mary's pain was in the bearing of us—her other Christs—on that awful day when the sun was darkened, the earth trembled, and graves gave up their dead. Mary became our Mother in that hour on Calvary when Jesus thought it was not enough to die for our salvation, but must add to the gift of eternal life the treasure of all His treasures—His Immaculate Mother, for our Mother.

In that hour in which Mary watched her Divine Son die, and in which she consented to become the Mother of all those who, through the Blessed Eucharist, would be incorporated into the Body of her Divine Son, there was added to Mary's titles still another. She—our House of Gold, our Morning Star, our Tower of Ivory—became, to angels and to men, the *Mother of Sorrows*.

Lam. 1;12: O all ye that pass by the way, attend, and see if there be any sorrow like to my sorrow...

Almost two thousand years have passed since the dark hours of Calvary and the dripping of the last drops of the Precious Blood of Jesus upon the earth. Two thousand years since the death of the God of Love!

Dying by the hand of His own people, Jesus still left to

them, and to us, two Gifts beyond recounting. Both these Gifts, His people, the Jews, have rejected. Their refusal of Him in the Blessed Sacrament is tragically consistent with their refusal of Him as the Son of God. Their refusal of Mary, the daughter of David, is tragically consistent with their refusal of Him as their King.

Almost two thousand years later, the Jews are in Jerusalem again. They are still without a King; still without a Messiah; still without the Son of God. Should they attempt again to rebuild the Temple—watch out for what is in store for the world! Mary has stayed the hand of God. She may not desire to stay it longer. The outraged Mother of a divine and doubly crucified Son is truly "terrible as an army set in array."[84]

The Faith passed from the Jews to the Gentiles. It passed from the East to the West. It built the civilization in which we live. The East became atrophied by schism; the West sundered by sects. Nations grew selfish; men cold, then selfish. Fear entered the world—with the revolt of Luther—craven, cowardly fear, removed from the holy, sanity-insuring fear of the Lord.

Fear bred compromise. "Live and let live; we have to get along; never discuss religion; never tell the whole truth; let people alone," were the pass-words of compromise. No matter that God be not glorified, nor Christ blazingly preached. Man must get along.

God was given a place and a time. The place was a parish church; the time was an hour, on a day—Sunday. The Blessed Sacrament became less and less the Bread of Life for all men, and Mary less and less the Queen-Mother of men's hearts. A new heresy was slipping in through the fog in men's minds.

---

[84] Cant. 6:3

And so, almost two thousand years after the death of Jesus, but one-sixth of the world is Catholic; but one-sixth confesses to the true Faith of Christ. And of that one-sixth, only a very, very small portion believe that either the death of Jesus, the Church He established, the Mother He gave us, or His own Body and Blood, Soul and Divinity in the Blessed Sacrament of His Love, are necessary for Salvation.

Queen of Angels, Gate of Heaven, Little Mother beneath the Cross, we know your heartbreak.

Epilogue

It gives me happiness to write, for those who have wanted to know, of what has become of us since October 28, 1949, the date at which our story ends in *The Loyolas and The Cabots*.[85] I am happy to tell this further story, even though briefly, because it is a recounting of the bounty and the protection of us by the Blessed Mother of God.

We who took part in the so-called Boston Heresy Case are, thanks to Our Lady, still together and intact. "Heresy," by the way, was an accusation made *by* us, not *of* us. Our accusation was substantiated by Father William Keleher's reply in the newspapers to the charge of the four professors.

We have lost of our number only six. Two dropped out, and four were dismissed, because, though we are not strict without reason, we do have our rules and decorum which must be lived up to. We do not know any religious group which has had so few casualties as Saint Benedict Center.

At this point, a reader may ask, "But are you a religious group?" The answer to that question reveals our secret. Yes, we are a religious community. We are, indeed, a religious order— perhaps more technically a religious congregation. Each of us has, by vow, dedicated his life to the preservation of the truths of his Holy Faith under the title of—Slaves of the Immaculate Heart of Mary.[86]

We took our vows and became Slaves of Our Lady's Immaculate Heart on the first of January, 1949, three months before we were disciplined by our Archbishop for continuing to

---

[85] A previous book of Sr. Catherine.

[86] In Latin, Mancipia Immaculati Cordis Mariae – M.I.C.M.

profess the defined doctrines of the Church on salvation. It was while Father Feeney was in correspondence with Father Vincent A. McCormick, S.J., the American Assistant to the General of the Jesuits, and while Father was pleading for a doctrinal hearing before his superiors. It was while three of the professors were under severe pressure by Boston College to give up both the Church's doctrine on salvation and their support of Father Feeney in upholding it.

We were beginning to realize the character of the battle before us, not only for the preservation of the sacred dogmas of the Church, but actually for their restoration. It was to prepare ourselves by prayer and discipline, and to secure graces enough to enable us to face such a battle, that we became a religious order.

It will be asked of us, "Who are you that you should take responsibility for the Church's doctrine?" Our answer to that, I hope I have brought out in this book. The answer is, as I wrote in the second chapter, that the sacred doctrine of our Holy Church is the responsibility of each Catholic, be he powerful or lowly, learned or unlettered, clergy or laity, rich or poor. Each of us is the Catholic Church. God's Truth belongs to each of us, and we are each responsible for it.

We live a community life, as Slaves of the Immaculate Heart of Mary, with hours of prayer, hours of study, and hours of work. Father Feeney and the young men who some day hope to be ordained priests live in one of our houses known to us as Sacred Heart Hall. Our girls who have dedicated their lives in singleness to Our Lord and Our Lady, live in a house which we call, among ourselves, Immaculate Heart Hall. Our families live in houses just below Sacred Heart Hall.

We are, during this interval under fire, waiting for the time when we can present our Order to the Holy See, as all Orders must eventually be presented. We know that many of the Orders in the Church whose work was most lasting and fruitful began under circumstances similar to ours. We know that many men and women who were later placed upon the rolls of the saints were at some time in their lives under the ban of interdict, and even excommunication. Saint Joan of Arc died excommunicated; Saint Ignatius of Constantinople died under threat of excommunication. We are not saints—though we pray we may be—and we are *not* excommunicated. We have offered our lives to God, and have consented to die, if need be, for our Holy Faith, in the saddest way (to our minds) that it is possible to die—under the ban even of excommunication.

We are waiting, then, to present our Order to the Holy See, to secure the blessing of our Holy Father, and to ask the Holy Father to foundation us as a permanent and abiding battalion in the army of our Holy Faith.

Father Feeney intends to get out, himself, a book on the whole controversy which is now at issue, and to show just how and where the theological teaching in this country started to go wrong, and where it should have been checked. Father has had, because of our Order, an extremely busy three years. Too, there is so much confusion both in the minds of the people and in the articles being written on the doctrine of salvation that until much of it subsides, Father thought it better to write a book in which his recollections could be clear and final. And so he chose to do a book about England—about London; in fact, about the center and core of all that England means to itself and to the world. Father's purpose in this book—by unanimous consent the most brilliant of any he has written—has been to show what happened to London when the Faith left it, and what is keeping the Faith from returning to London. Almost unknown to himself, Father Feeney has, in this delightful volume, *London Is a Place,* written the most beautiful apostrophe to the Blessed Virgin Mary that has yet come from his pen—which has been dedicated to no other service since the day Father first began to write.

Father's priestly heart and poet's nature, in spite of years of persecution, still finds it hard to believe men will give him back brutality and injustice in place of the trust he offers them. But they always do these days, and sometimes it is almost more than we can bear. The calumnies which have been deliberately spread about Father and Saint Benedict Center are so dreadful and unfounded that they could come only from a source which was very fearful that the truth should again be taught in its entirety.

And to that, our answer is—our Order; one hundred people vowed to the living of a religious life, for the preaching, teaching, and preservation of the doctrines of our Holy Faith. We have come together from nations and countries all over the world, and from different parts of the United States. We have some of the finest minds in the world, and certainly the bravest and stoutest hearts.

All are dedicated slaves of the Immaculate Heart of Mary.

DOCTORS OF THE CHURCH [87]

(Date is that of death)

(a) The Great Greek and Latin Doctors

1. Saint Athanasius, 373
2. Saint Basil, 379
3. Saint Gregory Nazianzen, 389
4. Saint John Chrysostom, 407
5. Saint Ambrose, 397
6. Saint Jerome, 420
7. Saint Augustine, 430
8. Saint Gregory the Great, 604

(b) Those Declared Doctors by the Popes since 1568

1. Saint Hilary of Poitiers, 368
2. Saint Ephrem the Syrian, 373
3. Saint Cyril of Jerusalem, 386
4. Saint Cyril of Alexandria, 444
5. Saint Peter Chrysologus, 450
6. Saint Leo the Great, 461
7. Saint Isidore of Seville, 636
8. Saint Bede the Venerable, 735
9. Saint John Damascene, 780
10. Saint Peter Damian, 1072
11. Saint Anselm, 1109
12. Saint Bernard, 1153
13. Saint Anthony of Padua, 1231
14. Saint Thomas Aquinas, 1274
15. Saint Bonaventure, 1274
16. Saint Albertus Magnus, 1280
17. Saint Peter Canisius, 1597
18. Saint John of the Cross, 1591
19. Saint Robert Bellarmine, 1621
20. Saint Francis de Sales, 1622

21. Saint Alphonsus Liguori, 1787

(c) Those Declared Doctors by the Popes since 1959

1. Saint Lawrence of Brindisi, 1619
2. Saint Teresa of Jesus (Avila), 1582
3. Saint Catherine of Siena, 1380
4. Saint Therese of Lisieux, 1897

---

[87] Since the writing of this book four more Doctors have been added to the Church. 1. Saint Lawrence of Brindisi, proclaimed Doctor, 1959. 2. Saint Teresa of Jesus (Avila), proclaimed first woman Doctor, Sept. 27, 1970. 3. Saint Catherine of Siena, proclaimed Doctor, Oct. 4, 1970. 4. Saint Therese of Lisieux, proclaimed Doctor, Oct. 20, 1997.

THE GENERAL, OR ECUMENICAL, COUNCILS [88]

1. Nicea (I) 325
2. Constantinople (1) 381
3. Ephesus, 431
4. Chalcedon 451
5. Constantinople (II) 553
6. Constantinople (III) 680
7. Nicea (II) 787
8. Constantinople (IV) 869-870
9. Lateran (I) 1123
10. Lateran (II) 1139
11. Lateran (III) 1179
12. Lateran (IV) 1215
13. Lyons (1) 1245
14. Lyons (II) 1274
15. Vienne 1311-1312
16. Constance 1414-1418
17. Basle-Florence 1431-1439
18. Lateran (V) 1512-1517
19. Trent 1545-1563
20. Vatican 1869-1870
21. Vatican II 1962-1965

THE APOSTOLIC FATHERS
(The immediate disciples of the Apostles)

Saint Polycarp of Smyrna (d. 155), disciple of Saint John the Evangelist.

Saint Papias of Hierapolis, disciple of Saint John and companion of Saint Polycarp.

Saint Ignatius of Antioch (d. 107), disciple of Saint Peter and Saint Paul. The first to call the Church "the Catholic Church."

Saint Clement of Rome, third successor of Saint Peter as Pope. Saint John was still alive during his pontificate.

---

[88] Since the writing of this book, the 21st Ecumenical Council of the Church took place, that being Vatican II (1962-65).

Gate of Heaven

EXTANT WRITINGS OF THE APOSTOLIC FATHERS

The *Didache* or "Teaching of the twelve apostles."

An *Epistle* attributed to Saint Barnabas.

Two *Epistles* of Saint Clement of Rome to the Corinthians.

Seven *Epistles* of Saint Ignatius of Antioch, to various Christian communities and to Polycarp.

The *Epistle* of Polycarp to the Philippians.

The *Epistle* of Diognetus, author unknown.

The *Explanations of Our Lord's Discourses,* by Papias.

The *Shepherd* of Hermas, who was the brother of Pope Saint Pius I.

Against Heresies and *The Demonstration of the Apostolic Teaching,* by Saint Irenaeus, who was a disciple of Saint Polycarp.

APPENDIX

The Only Way to Heaven

He that shall find me shall find life, and shall have salvation from the Lord. (**Prov. 8:35**)

What Holy Scripture Says

God "will have all men to be saved and to come to the knowledge of the truth." (1 Tim. 2:4)

"...Go ye into the whole world, and preach the gospel to every creature.

"He that believeth and is baptized, shall be saved: but he that believeth not shall be condemned." (Mark 16:15-16)

"Amen, amen I say to thee, unless a man be born again of water and the Holy Ghost, he cannot enter into the kingdom of God." (John 3:5)

"And I say to thee: that thou art Peter; and upon this rock I will build my church, and the gates of hell shall not prevail against it." (Matthew 16:18)

What the Popes Say

Ex Cathedra: * "There is but one universal Church of the faithful, outside of which no one at all can be saved." (Pope Innocent III, Fourth Lateran Council, 1215)

Ex Cathedra: "We declare, say, define, and pronounce that it is absolutely necessary for the salvation of every human creature to be subject to the Roman Pontiff." (Pope Boniface VIII, the Bull *Unam Sanctam*, 1302)

Ex Cathedra: "The most Holy Roman Church firmly believes,

---

* The Pope is said to speak *ex cathedra* when, in virtue of his supreme apostolic authority as the shepherd and teacher of all Christians, he defines a doctrine concerning faith or morals to be held by the whole Church.

professes, and preaches that none of those existing outside the Catholic Church, not only pagans, but also Jews and heretics and schismatics, can have a share in life eternal; but that they will go into the eternal fire which was prepared for the devil and his angels, unless before death they are joined with Her; and that so important is the unity of this ecclesiastical body that only those remaining within this unity can profit by the sacraments of the Church unto salvation, and they alone can receive an eternal recompense for their fasts, their almsgivings, their other works of Christian piety and the duties of a Christian soldier. No one, let his almsgiving be as great as it may, no one, even if he pour out his blood for the Name of Christ, can be saved, unless he remain within the bosom and the unity of the Catholic Church." (Pope Eugene IV, the Bull *Cantate Domino*, 1441)

What is a Dogma?

"A doctrine or a dogma of the Church is a truth which has been revealed by God and must be believed by all Catholics.

"Papal definition precludes any further interpretation of dogma. The Church has taught from its beginning that no matter how much a doctrine may be developed or meditated upon, never, never can its meaning in any way be changed. Despite all this, bishops, priests, theologians and canon lawyers in our day have insisted that distinctions be made with regard to the solemn doctrine 'Outside the Church there is No Salvation.'

"These distinctions are so involved, confused, fantastic and dishonest that the dogma finally has emerged—in the minds of the Faithful—as completely changed. To the straightforward question: Is there or is there not salvation outside the Catholic Church? The answer, after this manipulation of doctrine, would have to be: Yes, there is salvation outside the Catholic Church. We have arrived now at the exact opposite of the ex cathedra pronouncements of the Popes." (*Gate of Heaven*)

What the Saints Say

"No man can find salvation save in the Catholic Church. Outside the Catholic Church he can find everything except salvation. He can have dignities, he can have the Sacraments, can sing

'Alleluia,' answer 'Amen,' accept the Gospels, have faith in the Name of the Father, the Son and the Holy Ghost, and preach it, too, but never except in the Catholic Church can he find salvation." (Saint Augustine, 354-430)

"Hold most firmly, and do not doubt at all, that everyone baptized outside the Catholic Church cannot be made partaker of eternal life, if before the end of this earthly life he does not return to the Catholic Church and become incorporated with it....

"Hold most firmly, and do not doubt at all, that not only all the pagans, but also all the Jews, and all the heretics and schismatics who end the present life outside the Catholic Church, will go into the eternal fire, 'which was prepared for the devil and his angels.' (Matthew 25:41)" (Saint Fulgentius, 468-533)

"Outside of this communion (as outside of the Ark of Noah) there is absolutely no salvation for mortals: not to Jews or pagans, who never received the faith of the Church; not to heretics who, having received it, forsook or corrupted it; not to schismatics who left the peace and unity of the Church; finally neither to excommunicates who for any other serious cause deserved to be put away and separated from the body of the Church, like pernicious members.... For the rule of Cyprian and Augustine is certain: he will not have God for his Father who would not have the Church for his Mother." (Saint Peter Canisius, 1521-1597)

The Attack On the Mass

The Catholic Church, outside of which it is impossible to be saved, is being destroyed in our day by the same means that were used so successfully in the sixteenth century. Thomas Cranmer, the Archbishop of Canterbury at the time of the Protestant Revolt in England, knew that he could destroy the Faith if he could get rid of the Mass. Accordingly he replaced the Latin language—that great safeguard against the corruption of true doctrine—with the vernacular. He substituted a table for the altar in order to make of the Holy Sacrifice nothing more than a memorial meal. He changed the Canon of the Mass in order to get rid of the Real Presence of Our Lord in the Blessed Sacrament.

All the doctrines of the Catholic Faith are contained in the prayers of the Holy Sacrifice of the Mass. One of the reasons the Liberals of our day have been trying to change our traditional liturgy is that it safeguards the dogma of No Salvation Outside the Catholic Church.

Pope Saint Pius V, in order to protect forever the Holy Sacrifice of the Mass and the dogmas it embodies, issued in the sixteenth century the proclamation *Quo Primum.*

This says in part:

> Specifically, do we warn all persons in authority of whatever dignity or rank, Cardinals not excluded, and command them as a matter of strict obedience never to use or permit any ceremonies or Mass prayers other than the ones contained in this Missal....
>
> At no time in the future can a priest, whether secular or order priest, ever be forced to use any other way of saying Mass. And in order once and for all to preclude any scruples of conscience and fear of ecclesiastical penalties and censures, we declare herewith that it is by virtue of our Apostolic authority that we decree and prescribe that this present order and decree of ours is to last in perpetuity, and never at a future date can it be revoked or amended legally....
>
> And if, nevertheless, anyone would dare attempt any action contrary to this order of ours, handed down for all times, let him know that he has incurred the wrath of Almighty God, and of the Blessed Apostles Peter and Paul.

INDEX